Diversity at School

Anne Lodge and Kathleen Lynch (Editors)

Contributors:
Eilís Barry
Marie Clarke
Joan Hanafin
Mairín Ke
Anne Lo
Kathleen
Rose Ma
Michael S.

First published 2004
by the
Institute of Public Administration
57–61 Lansdowne Road
Dublin 4

for the
Equality Authority
2 Clonmel Street
Dublin 2

British Library Cataloguing in Publication Data

ISBN-10: 1 904541 19 4
ISBN-13: 978 1 904541 19 6

The opinions of the editors or contributors do not necessarily reflect the position of the Equality Authority.

Cover design by Language, Dublin
Print origination by M & J Graphics, Dublin
Printed in Ireland by Future Print Ltd, Dublin

Contents

Tables

v

About the Authors

Anne Lodge is a member of the Education Department at NUI Maynooth, where she lectures in Sociology of Education. She is co-author with Kathleen Lynch of *Equality and Power in Schools: Redistribution, Recognition and Representation*. She is co-editor with Jim Deegan and Dympna Devine of *Primary Voices: Equality, Diversity and Childhood in Irish Primary Schools*.

Kathleen Lynch is Professor of Equality Studies at University College Dublin. She has written extensively on equality and education. Her recent publications include *Equality in Education; Equality and Power in Schools: Redistribution, Recognition and Representation* (co-authored with Anne Lodge); *Inside Classrooms: The Teaching and Learning of Mathematics in Social Context* (co-authored with Maureen Lyons, Sean Close, Philip Boland and Emer Sheerin); and *Equality: From Theory to Action* (co-authored with John Baker, Sara Cantillon and Judy Walsh).

Eilís Barry BL is legal advisor to the Equality Authority and is head of its legal section. Prior to joining the Equality Authority, she practised as a barrister for fifteen years, specialising in employment and discrimination cases. She is co-editor, with Cathryn Costello, of *Equality in Diversity: The New Equality Directives*.

Marie Clarke is a member of the Education Department at University College Dublin, where she lectures in Curriculum Studies and Adult Education. She is engaged in a wide range of research on adult education, citizenship and education for refugees and asylum seekers.

Joan Hanafin is a member of the Education Department at University College Cork, where she lectures in Research Methods, Curriculum and Sociology of Education. She is co-author of *Gender Politics and Exploring Masculinities in Irish Education: Teachers, Materials and the Media* with Máirtín Mac an Ghaill and Paul Conway.

Mairín Kenny is an educational researcher and training consultant. She has authored and co-authored articles, books and reports on Travellers and education, intercultural issues in education and education for those with disabilities.

Rose Malone is a member of the Education Department at NUI Maynooth, where she lectures in Curriculum Studies. She is currently engaged in research into early school leaving and science education.

Michael Shevlin is a member of the Education Department at Trinity College Dublin, where he lectures on Inclusive Education. He has authored and co-authored articles, books and reports on education for learners with disabilities.

Foreword

The Equality Authority has a broad mandate under the equality legislation to promote equality of opportunity and to combat discrimination. The field of education has been identified as a core focus in the work of the Equality Authority. The Employment Equality Acts prohibit discrimination in the workplace, which is relevant for staff in educational establishments. The Equal Status Acts prohibit discrimination in the provision of goods and services, accommodation and education. The Department of Education and Science is a significant service provider and the Acts include specific provisions in relation to educational establishments.

Diversity at School provides an important foundation for the work of the Equality Authority in the area of education. It gathers together a wide range of sources of knowledge and research on equality and education and it maps out a range of equality issues in education for each area covered by the equality legislation. It will be a key resource for the Equality Authority as it develops its programme of work in this area.

Diversity at School is a unique and valuable initiative. It is unique in encompassing all nine grounds covered by the equality legislation – gender, marital status, family status, age, disability, sexual orientation, race, religion and membership of the Traveller community – in a single study. It is valuable in its identification of a broad range of issues that need to be addressed in schools and other educational institutions if equality is to be effectively promoted in a context of diversity.

The work of the Equality Authority combines both enforcement and developmental strategies. Enforcement work includes support for individuals who feel they have been discriminated against in cases that have a strategic importance. In 2003 the Equality Authority had seventy-eight legal case files under the Equal Status Act in relation to educational establishments; it also dealt with 124 queries to its Public Information Centre in this area. The legal case files represent 10 per cent of the total Equality Authority case files worked on during 2003 under the Equal

ix

Status Act, and educational establishments were the second-highest area of case work (after licensed premises). The case files covered issues of access by Travellers and pupils with disabilities to schools and to particular subject areas, of school uniform and dress code issues on the gender ground, of access by members of particular religions to schools of another religious ethos, of access to non-denominational schooling and of harassment on the sexual orientation ground. A significant number of these cases were settled prior to hearing. This reflects an openness on the part of schools to implement necessary change. However, many parents have also shown a reluctance to take cases.

The developmental work of the Equality Authority has included research, such as this report. Information strategies to assist schools and other educational institutions have been implemented. An example of this work was the joint preparation and dissemination with the Department of Education and Science of the booklet *Schools and the Equal Status Act*. Joint initiatives have been taken with the Association of Secondary Teachers Ireland (ASTI) and the Irish National Teachers' Organization (INTO) to support debate and exploration of new practices in educational establishments to promote equality and combat discrimination. School development planning and school evaluation templates have been a particular focus for work with the Department of Education and Science and its associated bodies, with the aim of supporting the equality dimension in these areas.

In this work the Equality Authority has promoted the goal of the inclusive school, which prevents and combats discrimination. The inclusive school respects, values and accommodates diversity across all nine grounds in the equality legislation. It makes reasonable accommodation for students with disabilities and seeks positive experiences, a sense of belonging and positive outcomes for all students across the nine grounds. Outcomes include access, participation, personal development and achieving education credentials. The inclusive school also supports participation in decision making by a diversity of pupils. It has a similar concern for and focus on diversity among staff. Equality and education legislation usefully underpin and advance this goal of the inclusive school.

Diversity at School identifies a broad range of issues that need to be addressed if the inclusive school is to become a widespread reality. It stimulates optimism in identifying the current good practice that is in place alongside the significant challenges that continue to be posed by this ambition for equality. It identifies valuable strategies for change that can be implemented now and over the coming years. The Equality Authority looks forward to making its contribution to the implementation of these strategies and to working with the many stakeholders in the field of education to support their implementation.

The Equality Authority is grateful to the authors of the different chapters. Particular gratitude is due to Anne Lodge and Kathleen Lynch, who have edited the overall publication and contributed to its content. Their contribution in relation to equality and education is already well established and this publication marks another important contribution to their usual high standard. Finally, gratitude is also due to Cathal Kelly and Laurence Bond of the Equality Authority, who both managed and contributed to this project.

Niall Crowley

Niall Crowley
Chief Executive Officer
Equality Authority
September 2004

Chapter 1
Introduction

1.1 The equality debate about education in Ireland

Education is one of the major social institutions in our society, with almost 1 million people involved annually in education programmes from early childhood to later adulthood. Recent debate in Irish education has focused on the impact of socio-economic status on rates of access and participation. Since the publication of the *Investment in Education Report* in 1966 (Department of Education 1966), numerous studies and reports have been commissioned documenting differences across social classes and socio-economic groups in rates of participation. Among the most notable of these has been the series of studies commissioned by the Higher Education Authority (Clancy and Benson 1979; Clancy 1982, 1988, 1995; Clancy and Wall 2000; Clancy 2002) that document systematic differences across socio-economic groups in rates of participation in higher education.

Although vital for the promotion of equality generally, the focus on socio-economic status has overshadowed the impact of other differences. While gender has been the subject of inquiry in studies by the Economic and Social Research Institute (ESRI) (Hannan *et al.* 1983, 1996; Smyth 2001) as well as other commentators (Lynch 1989), it has not been given the same analytical attention as socio-economic factors in other studies. Other social differences have received relatively little research attention. The impact of statuses such as ethnicity (including membership of the Traveller community), family and marital status, sexual orientation and religion have been the subject of relatively little discussion and analysis. However, there has been a growing body of work in recent years on disability (Farrell 1995; Kenny *et al.* 2000) and age (HEEU 1996; Fleming and Murphy 1997; Lynch 1999). The Higher Education Equality Unit (HEEU 1997) has also been active in encouraging research and debate on Black and minority ethnic groups in higher education. Public awareness of the presence in Ireland of Black and minority ethnic groups, including those seeking

1

asylum, those granted refugee status and those who come to Ireland as migrant workers, has resulted in a developing interest in research studies focusing on the experiences of specific Black and minority ethnic groups in the compulsory education sector (Keogh and Whyte 2002).

Significant data deficits are an impediment to an effective focus on equality in education for groups covered by the equality legislation. The Department of Education and Science's annual *Statistical Reports* provide no systematic data on the social groups covered in the equality legislation with the exception of gender. Furthermore, data on students in adult and community education is not recorded on any systematic basis nationally. While the colleges of higher education do collect profile data on entrants, this is not standardised and it is not inclusive of most of the grounds named in the equality Acts.

The lack of analysis of differences arising from disability, age, sexual orientation and other statuses in relation to education is accompanied by other limitations in research and policy. These include a narrow focus on distributive justice in terms of equal formal rights. That is, justice and equality in education are often seen only in terms of who gets access to or participates in schooling or further or higher education. Most of the debate assumes that education is an unproblematic good that is there to be accessed and availed of by all (Connell 1993; Lynch 1999).

A more comprehensive framework for considering equality has been outlined by the National Economic and Social Forum (NESF 2002). This suggests that equality should be seen in terms of four interrelated sets of issues:

• redistribution, which is concerned with access to resources and benefits

• political equality, which is concerned with participation in decision making and overcoming inequalities in power between different groups

• the affective domain, which is concerned with relationships of love, care and solidarity

• socio-cultural equality, which is concerned with respect for and recognition of differences between people and groups in society and valuing, accommodating and celebrating these differences.

This report looks at issues that arise across this framework, although there is a particular focus on the socio-cultural equality element above.

In terms of curriculum, modes of assessment and pedagogical and organisational practice, the potential for education to be exclusive and excluding in its treatment of different types of students has been largely ignored in discussions of equality in education in Ireland. The (legitimate) concern with getting people into education has been paralleled with a limited focus on their experience of and achievements in education. The fact that Ireland has such a poor educational profile in terms of adult literacy and numeracy and in terms of retention in the noncompulsory phase of schooling is a telling indicator of the severe limitations of this approach to equality adopted even in the targeted area of socio-economic status (Morgan *et al.* 1997; OECD 2000).

The reluctance to engage with issues of difference in education is also indicative of other influences on education. Irish education is largely denominationally controlled at primary and second level. The daily operations of most schools assume that students are Christian, if not Roman Catholic, thereby raising important questions about how differences in religious beliefs are accommodated in schools. Given the teaching of the main Christian churches on sexual orientation in particular, it is almost impossible for those who are openly gay, lesbian or bisexual to feel that they have parity of status with heterosexual persons in religious-controlled schools, either as students or as teachers. While there is no doubt that some schools afford recognition to persons of minority sexual orientation, the official teaching of most of the major religions precludes this. The religious control of schools in a predominantly state-funded system presents serious challenges to the pursuit of equality for particular minorities in education.

Analysing and addressing differences in policy terms is also hindered by the profoundly consensual culture that dominates the debates about education in Ireland (Lynch 1987). Even though Ireland has never been homogenous culturally or politically, there was a deep and persistent attempt to create an image of cultural and political homogeneity in the post-independence years. A culture of manufactured homogeneity developed that became almost incontestable; daring to name differences was seen as a challenge to authority, a deviant act, rather than a statement of fact. Differences around disability, ethnicity, beliefs, etc. became subsumed and suppressed in a society in which all were deemed to be the same. As historians have indicated (Coolahan 1981), the state project of political and cultural cohesion and homogenisation was realised in great part through education, hence the neglect, and even negation, of difference in educational life.

The denial of difference at the cultural level has been paralleled by institutionalising differences in organisational terms. Irish schools remain among the most segregated in Europe. Students with disabilities, especially those with learning disabilities, have been segregated into special schools; teenage Travellers have been segregated into training centres; girls are still educated separately from boys in many secondary schools; and different religious groups are still educated separately.

Another constraint on the recognition of difference in education has been the way in which power and control are exercised. At a national level, power is exercised among a small number of hugely influential actors, most notably the teacher unions, the Churches, the Vocational Educational Committees and the Department of Education and Science itself (Drudy and Lynch 1993). (The OECD (1991) has suggested that the teacher unions are *the* most powerful players.) Most major policy committees, review bodies, curriculum boards, etc. are constituted from the prevailing interest groups. Although some groups have been consulted on an *ad hoc* basis for particular projects, there is no place for consistent inclusion of groups representing minorities or even majorities (such as the National Women's Council of Ireland); in policy-making terms, much of education decision making is a closed shop. At school level, parents have a formal role in school management and students have a right to be informed of the school's activities. At post-primary level this includes encouraging the establishment of student councils to promote student interests. However, this involvement of parents and students at school level is not required to reflect diversity in the school community across grounds such as ethnicity, membership of the Traveller community, family status, marital status, sexual orientation, disability or religion.

1.2 The structure of the Irish education system

One of the notable aspects of Irish education, at all levels, is the extent of private ownership and control in both the compulsory and noncompulsory sectors. The high level of private ownership and control is unparalleled in comparable state-funded systems (Clancy 1999). The

---

[1]Under the Education (Welfare) Act 2000, young people are obliged to engage in full-time education from the age of six up to either the age of sixteen or three years of attendance at post-primary education.

compulsory[1] sector (primary and post-primary), particularly at post-primary level, comprises both state-owned and privately owned institutions. The great majority of the latter are in denominational control. The relatively high proportion by international standards of single-sex institutions within the compulsory sector is one consequence of the origins and traditions of denominationally controlled schools. Over 90 per cent of primary schools are denominationally controlled and are mainly Roman Catholic. However, since the mid-1980s the majority of newly established primary schools have been multidenominational schools or Gaelscoileanna, representing a change in traditional patterns (Tovey and Share 2000).

While there are some sectoral differences in levels of funding at primary and second level, all schools (with the exception of the small number of fee-paying primary schools) are in receipt of most of their funding for capital and current costs from the Exchequer (Drudy and Lynch 1993). In addition, a standardised curriculum is offered across all recognised schools, with all students at second level being prepared for public examinations. Despite the standardisation of curricula, there is a considerable degree of local discretion in the implementation of policy on curriculum and related matters (Smyth and Hannan 2000). However, the introduction of new legislation relating directly or indirectly to education in recent years (the Education Act 1998, the Education (Welfare) Act 2000, the Equal Status Act 2000) has brought about a change in the relative levels of freedom that schools have to control all their own internal practices. The universities and higher education bodies are also operating under legislation (the Universities Act 1997, the Equal Status Acts 2000 to 2004) with equality provisions.

The compulsory sector of education has experienced relative under-resourcing compared with that documented in other developed countries. Ireland was ranked last out of fourteen countries in its funding of both primary and second-level education in a study by the OECD (2000). While funding for the tertiary sector is more generous in comparative terms internationally, Ireland is still ranked sixteenth out of twenty-four countries by the OECD (2000). Moreover, the funding for tertiary education declined in the late 1990s (Archer 2001).

Noncompulsory education is also characterised by a mixture of public and private ownership and control. The tertiary sector comprises a range of state-funded universities (and their constituent colleges), institutes of technology and teacher education colleges[2] alongside a growing number of private third-level providers. The development of private tertiary institutions is not the only example of increasing marketisation of the Irish education system. At upper second level, private, fee-paying 'grind' schools have also been established, with the primary objective of getting students high grades (points) to enter third-level education (Tovey and Share 2000). At the same time, an unknown number of young people seek private grinds in individual subjects.

The two sectors that attract the lowest levels of funding are those catering for preschool-age children and for adult learners. *Ready to Learn: White Paper on Early Childhood Education* recognises that state provision of preschool education[3] in Ireland compares poorly with other European Union member states (Department of Education and Science 1999f). Adult and community education is a hugely diverse sector and is one that has been subject to relative neglect (McMinn 2000; Tovey and Share 2000).

1.3 Structure of the report

Assessing the extent and nature of inequality in education would be a mammoth task in and of itself. To be comprehensive it would require a detailed appraisal of practices, processes and outcomes at all levels of education, including preschool, first and second level, further and higher education and adult and community education. By definition, such a task is beyond the scope of this report.

What is presented here is a general overview of the issues that accompany diversity at school and in other educational institutions across the grounds named in the equality legislation. Because of the limitations of data availability, the review is limited in a number of cases, most conspicuously in relation to marital status but also in relation to other areas such as ethnicity, membership of the Traveller community and sexual orientation.

Chapter 2 presents an overview of the equality legislation and draws attention to other laws, including some elements of the education

---

[2] Teacher education colleges are denominationally controlled (Drudy and Lynch 1993; Tovey and Share 2000).

[3] There is some state provision of preschool education in Ireland, which is targeted at those who are deemed to be disadvantaged, including those living in areas designated as socio-economically disadvantaged (the Early Start programme), members of the Traveller community and those assessed as having special learning needs (Drudy and Lynch 1993; Murphy 2000).

legislation. In the following chapters we present a review of the equality issues for the different grounds named in the equality legislation in terms of presence and participation and of diversity and recognition. We examine concerns regarding harassment experienced as a consequence of diversity and status and look briefly at employment equality issues. Most attention is focused on the compulsory sectors of education given their particular importance. (Under the Education (Welfare) Act 2000, young people between the ages of six and sixteen are required to attend school unless satisfactory alternative arrangements for their education have been made.) We identify good practice initiatives in each case. The concluding chapter offers a series of general recommendations.

Except for Chapter 4, which deals with two grounds, each chapter focuses on a single ground. It must also be remembered that people hold multiple identities and can be covered by more than one ground. Likewise, case work under the equality legislation can be on more than one ground. For example, a case on the gender ground may also raise issues on the marital status or family status grounds. Our understanding of the issues that arise from the multiple and intersecting identities that people have has been developed by research commissioned by the equality and human rights bodies in Britain, Ireland and Northern Ireland (Zappone 2003).

What needs to be kept in mind throughout the report is the over-powering influence of economic forces (socio-economic and social class) on the effective participation of all groups. It is those from the lowest socio-economic groups who experience the greatest disadvantage within any given status group (Hannan *et al.* 1996; Lynch 1999; Smyth 1999). As social background is not named in either the Employment Equality Acts 1998 and 2004 or the Equal Status Acts 2000 to 2004, it is not part of what we address here; however, it remains a crucial equality concern in education (Blossfeld and Shavit 1993).

The completion of this report has been the result of collective work by all of those involved. The editors wish to acknowledge their particular contributions to different chapters and sections: Anne Lodge and Kathleen Lynch, Chapters 1, 3 and 11; Eilís Barry, Chapter 2; Joan Hanafin, family status in Chapter 4; Kathleen Lynch, marital status in Chapter 4; Anne Lodge, Chapters 5 and 6; Marie Clarke and Rose Malone, Chapter 7; Marie Clarke and Anne Lodge, Chapter 8; Mairín Kenny and Michael Shevlin, Chapter 9; and Mairín Kenny and Anne Lodge, Chapter 10.

Chapter 2
Legislation – An Overview

2.1 The equality legislation
The main body of legislation governing equality and discrimination is the Employment Equality Acts and the Equal Status Acts. Both of these pieces of legislation have been amended since they were originally enacted, most significantly by the Equality Act 2004. The amended Acts are sometimes referred to in legal contexts as the Employment Equality Acts 1998 and 2004 and the Equal Status Acts 2000 to 2004, but in this book the date in the title of either of these Acts is not cited unless it is required by the particular context. Although the legislation applies to most employment situations and to the provision of a wide range of goods and services (including the provision of accommodation), the focus here is on its relevance to education.

Discrimination
Both the Employment Equality Acts and the Equal Status Acts prohibit discrimination on nine grounds, which are gender, family status, marital status, sexual orientation, religion, age, race, disability and membership of the Traveller community. Discrimination is the treatment of a person in a less favourable way than another person has been or would be treated in a comparable situation. The legislation prohibits discrimination, including indirect discrimination and discrimination by association.

Sexual harassment and harassment
Harassment occurs when a person subjects the victim to any form of unwanted conduct related to any of the discriminatory grounds that has the purpose or effect of violating a person's dignity and creating an intimidating, hostile, degrading, humiliating or offensive environment for the victim.

Sexual harassment occurs when a person subjects the victim to any form of unwanted verbal, nonverbal or physical conduct of a sexual nature that

8

has the purpose or effect of violating a person's dignity and creating an intimidating, hostile, degrading, humiliating or offensive environment for the victim.

In both cases the unwanted conduct may include acts, requests, spoken words, gestures or the production, display or circulation of written words, pictures or other materials.

Sexual harassment and harassment of an employee are prohibited in the workplace or in the course of employment. The prohibition applies to such conduct committed by another employee, by the employer or by clients, customers or other business contacts of the employer.

Sexual harassment and harassment of a student at an educational establishment is prohibited. Principals, teachers and others in positions of responsibility in a school may not harass or sexually harass students at a school or anyone who has applied for admission. A person who is responsible for the operation of any place that is an educational establishment (or where goods, facilities or services are offered to the public, or a person who provides accommodation) must ensure that any person who has a right to be there is not sexually harassed or harassed. The 'responsible person' will be liable for the sexual harassment or harassment unless he or she took reasonably practicable steps to prevent it.

The Equality Authority has published a Code of Practice on Sexual Harassment and Harassment at Work (S.I. no. 78 of 2002).

Liability of employers
Under the equality legislation, employers are liable for anything done by an employee in the course of his or her employment, unless the employer can prove that he or she took reasonably practicable steps to prevent the discrimination.

Reasonable accommodation
Under the Equal Status Acts, service providers, including educational establishments, are required to provide reasonable accommodation to meet the needs of a service user or student who has a disability. An exemption can apply if the reasonable accommodation would give rise to anything more than a nominal cost.

Under the Employment Equality Acts, employers are required to provide reasonable accommodation to meet the needs of an employee who has a disability. An exemption can apply if the reasonable accommodation would impose a disproportionate burden on the employer.

Positive action
The Employment Equality Acts permit positive action measures that seek to achieve full equality in practice. The Equal Status Acts allow positive action measures that target disadvantaged students or who have special needs. (The term 'special needs' in the Equal Status Acts has a broader meaning than the same term usually has in an educational context.)

Equal Status Acts
The Equal Status Acts cover:

- buying, selling or renting a wide variety of goods

- a wide range of services, including public services like health, welfare and services provided by the Department of Education and Science (schools may also be service providers to parents)

- buying, selling or renting accommodation (this would include a school letting a hall for local activities)

- educational establishments.

If something is required by another law, for example the Education Act or a court order, the provisions of the Equal Status Acts cannot be construed as prohibiting it. However, if an organisation (such as a school) has any discretion about how it meets a legal requirement, then the way it does that must not breach the Equal Status Acts.

Education and the Equal Status Acts
The Equal Status Acts have specific provisions on educational establishments. They cover preschool services, primary or post-primary schools, adult, continuing or further education, universities and other third-level or higher-level institutions. They also include public and private educational establishments.

An educational establishment may not discriminate in relation to:

- the admission or terms or conditions of admission

- the access of any student to any course, facility or benefit

- any other term or condition of participation

- the expulsion of a student or other sanction.

There are a number of exemptions that are relevant to particular grounds and these are mentioned in the relevant chapters in this book.

Employment Equality Acts
The Employment Equality Acts apply to advertising, equal pay, access to employment, vocational training and work experience, the terms and conditions of employment, promotion or regrading, the classification of posts, dismissal and collective agreements. The Acts apply to full-time, part-time and temporary employees, to public- and private-sector employment and to vocational training bodies, employment agencies, trade unions and professional bodies. They also extend to the self-employed and partnerships. There are a number of exemptions that are relevant to particular grounds and these are mentioned in the relevant chapters in this book.

2.2 The education legislation
There are a number of provisions in other education legislation that are relevant.

Schools have a number of duties under the Education Act 1998. They must promote equality of opportunity for male and female students. This would include sports and extracurricular activities. Schools are also required to use their available resources to ensure that the educational needs of all students, including those with a disability or other special educational needs, are identified and provided for. Schools are required to have an admissions policy and this must provide for maximum accessibility to the school. The board of management must ensure that the admissions policy respects the principle of equality.

School boards of management must prepare a school plan, which must state the objectives of the school relating to equality of access to and participation in the school. It must also set out the measures the school will take to achieve these equality objectives.

Under the Education (Welfare) Act 2000 school boards of management have to prepare a code of behaviour in respect of students. This code must specify the standards of behaviour that students are required to observe. In meeting this requirement, a school could contribute to meeting its requirements under the Equal Status Acts by naming the nine grounds in the equality legislation in its code of behaviour, by stating that sexual harassment or harassment on these grounds are prohibited and by setting out policies and procedures to prevent and respond to such harassment.

2.3 The Constitution

The Constitution contains a number of provisions that are relevant to education and equality. Among these are the equality provisions in Article 40.1, the personal rights referred to in Article 40.3 and the provisions on education and the family in Article 42.

2.4 EU directives

The Equality Act 2004 aims to implement three European Union directives: the Race Directive, the Framework Employment Directive and the Amended Gender Equal Treatment Directive. The Race Directive explicitly applies to education. The Framework Employment Directive contains provisions that are relevant to the grounds of age, disability, religion and sexual orientation. The amended Gender Equal Treatment Directive imposes a duty on the state to promote gender employment equality, which extends to the employment of teachers. The provisions of the directives take precedence over Irish legislation, including the Education Act, the Employment Equality Acts and the Equal Status Acts.

Chapter 3
Gender

3.1 Introduction and background information

Discrimination on the gender ground under the equality legislation occurs when one person is treated in a comparable situation less favourably than another person because of their gender, that is, being a man or a woman. On foot of an EU court ruling, it would also afford protection to transsexual people. Some of the particular provisions and exemptions that apply to the gender ground to be found in the Employment Equality Acts and the Equal Status Acts, respectively, are given in Tables 1 and 2.

Table 1. Some provisions in the Employment Equality Acts relating to gender

---

Additional definition of discrimination
Discrimination on the gender ground also occurs where, on a ground related to her pregnancy or maternity leave, a woman employee is treated contrary to any statutory requirement less favourably than another employee is, has been or would be treated.

Exemptions include
Treatment that confers benefit on women in connection with pregnancy and maternity, including breastfeeding, is allowed.

Given the scope and range of educational services within the state it is not possible to review gender equality issues within them in any systematic way in this brief résumé. Moreover, as gender equality in education is a very complex subject involving issues of power and resources and affective as well as socio-cultural or recognition issues, it is not possible to review research on gender equality in any complete sense here.

Table 2. Some provisions in the Equal Status Acts relating to gender

---

Exemptions include

Primary and secondary schools may be for one gender only.

Institutions established for providing training to ministers of a particular religion may admit students of only one gender.

Educational establishments can provide different treatment on the gender ground in relation to the provision or organisation of sporting events or facilities, but only to the extent that the differences are reasonably necessary having regard to the nature of the facilities or events.

3.2 Presence and participation issues

Table 3 summarises the most recent data available on enrolment in education broken down by age and gender. Almost all young people between the ages of five and fourteen are at school. This is not the case for those under five and from the age of fifteen up, and here there are noticeable differences in enrolment by gender, with higher participation rates for females than for males.

Early school leaving is heavily concentrated among students of both genders from working-class backgrounds, although it is especially strong among young men from such backgrounds. Of those who drop out early from school without qualifications, almost two-thirds (64 per cent) are male (McCoy *et al.* 1999). This is reflected in participation in post-school second chance programmes, such as Youthreach, where approximately 60 per cent of trainees are male and 40 per cent are female (Department of Education and Science 2000a).

The ESRI *School Leavers' Survey* for 1998 shows that overall, 45 per cent of female school leavers progressed to further study, compared with 34 per cent of males. Patterns of participation in further and higher education vary across different sectors (McCoy *et al.* 1999).

The Post-Leaving Certificate sector currently represents one of the biggest growth areas in Irish education, with 23,823 participants in 1998–9. Of these, 71 per cent were women (Department of Education and Science 2000d). The pattern of participation in vocational training is somewhat different. The 1998 figures show that of the 11,537 trainees in the area of Specific Skills Training, 4,878 (42 per cent) were women and in the area of

Table 3. Estimated participation rates in full-time education by age and gender

Age	Male Enrolment (%)	Female Enrolment (%)
4	47.1	51.4
5	98.7	101.1*
6–14	100.5*	101.1*
15	95.1	98.2
16	88.2	94.8
17	73.8	86.7
18	53.7	71.0
19	40.0	56.3
20	33.7	45.4
21	25.9	30.9

*Some figures exceed 100 per cent because the data is based on estimates of population.

Source: Department of Education and Science Statistical Reports 2000/2001

Traineeship (total 1,265) 46 per cent were women. In the area of Standards-based Apprenticeship, however, less than 1 per cent (50 out of 7,147) trainees were women (Department of Education and Science 2000a).

Overall, women slightly outnumber men in the higher education sector, especially in the universities (Clancy and Wall 2000). There are more men than women in certificate and diploma programmes, however, reflecting the concentration of these courses in the institutes of technology. Men also outnumber women at PhD level (Lynch 1999).

At second level, females tend to outperform males in public examinations (Hannan *et al.* 1996). This aggregate finding, however, is likely to conceal social class and ethnic differences in performance. Data from England suggests that it is boys from working-class and some minority ethnic backgrounds who perform least well (Arnot *et al.* 1998).

The gender differential is different at third level, where males tend to obtain a disproportionately high number of higher-level awards. A study by Lynch *et al.* (1999) undertaken for the Points Commission found that while 39 per cent of men received a 1 or 2.I award, only 29 per cent of women received such awards, although women entered higher education with a higher average Leaving Certificate grade point average than men.

The gender disparities favouring males were greatest in the humanities, where men were 1.8 times more likely to be awarded a 1 or 2.I grade. The reasons for gender disparities in performance at second and third level have not been examined in Ireland, but they need further research.

Gender segregation and subject provision and choice

It is impossible to discuss gender equality in Irish education without recognising the important role played by gender-segregated schooling at both primary and post-primary levels and the related issue of gendered patterns of subject uptake.

Unlike the situation internationally, where coeducation is the norm for the vast majority of schools, single-sex schooling remains relatively commonplace in Ireland, particularly at second level, where 30 per cent of primary school children and 39 per cent of second-level students are in single-sex schools (Table 4).

Table 4. Gender composition of primary and post-primary schools in Ireland

School type	Proportion of all schools	Proportion of all pupils
Primary schools		
Single-sex girls	8.9	15.4
Single-sex boys	5.0	14.8
Coeducational	86.0	69.9
Post-primary schools		
Single-sex girls	20.0	22.5
Single-sex boys	15.8	16.0
Coeducational	64.2	61.5

Source: Department of Education and Science Statistics Section, figures for 2000–01

While the Department of Education and Science is actively supportive of coeducation, it cannot compel any single-sex institution to enrol both female and male students. The Equal Status Acts specifically recognise the right of single-sex primary and post-primary schools to continue as such. What this means in effect is that gender-segregated education has been protected in Irish law. While this does not create any evident inequalities in terms of access to good-quality education, it does mean that a very large proportion of people cannot avail of the day-to-day learning about gender relations that takes place in coeducational environments. It also means that certain types of subjects in second level are more likely to be available to girls than to boys and vice versa because of the gendered character of subject provision in single-sex schools.

A study commissioned by the Council for the Status of Women and the Department of Education in the early 1980s, *Schooling and Sex Roles* (Hannan *et al.* 1983), documented a significant degree of gender differentiation in both the provision of and access to subjects with traditional gendered associations. Gender equality issues in education have since been the focus of a significant number of intervention programmes and action research initiated by the Department of Education and Science to address such issues. Some examples include the *TENET* project, which included a subproject entitled *Equal Opportunities for Girls and Boys in the Primary School Curriculum*. This latter project was continued and expanded in the Gender Equity Action Research Project. Examples of other projects include *Intervention Project in Physics and Chemistry* and the *EU Teacher Education Action Research Project*.

Despite the interventions there is evidence that single-sex schooling does constrain students' subject choices in particularly gendered ways. Only a few boys' schools offer Home Economics to students throughout their second-level careers: just 4 (out of 146) offered it at Junior Certificate level in 1998–9 compared with 163 out of 165 girls' schools. Music is also highly gendered in its provision: 61 boys' schools and 150 girls' schools offered Junior Certificate Music. On the other hand, few girls' schools offer the technological subjects (such as Technical Graphics or Materials Technology): in 1998–9 only 2 girls' schools offered Materials Technology (Wood), while 15 offered Technical Graphics; the comparable figures for boys' schools were 92 and 117, respectively. The implications of segregation, therefore, are significant in terms of subject access (Department of Education and Science 2000d). Girls' and boys' choices are limited indirectly by the segregated system. While student choice is undoubtedly still a major factor in determining choices irrespective of availability (Hannan *et al.* 1983, 1996), nonetheless choices are further constrained when the options are not available in the first instance.

A study within the coeducational sector conducted during the early 1990s found that gender differentiation played a part in the way schools allocated students to subjects at second level (Hannan *et al.* 1996).

However, there are certain subjects where it plays a relatively significant role, namely in the technological subjects. The authors observe, however, that schools may currently be using more subtle methods of differentiating in subject access according to gender, such as discouraging nontraditional entrants to particular fields, operating timetabling practices that polarise gender choices or simply not encouraging students to make choices that are nontraditional in gender terms. Lynch and Lodge (2002) found evidence of these latter practices in their research on schools.

The net effect of the gender-segregated character of schooling, of the gendering of provision in certain subjects in some coeducational schools and of gendered choices regardless of school type is that there are fields of knowledge and understanding that are dominated by one gender group in schools. At Leaving Certificate level in 1997–8, only 5 per cent, 6 per cent and 7 per cent, respectively, of those doing Engineering, Technical Drawing and Construction Studies were female. While girls constitute 51 per cent of those taking Chemistry, they constitute only 25 per cent of Physics students. On the other hand, only 6 per cent of those taking Home Economics (both the Social and Scientific syllabus and the General syllabus) and 17 per cent of those taking Music were male (Department of Education and Science, *Statistical Report 1997/98*, cited in Galligan 2000: 59–60). While the gendering of subject choices is not unique to Ireland, it does pose questions as to how real the equality of access to technological subjects is for girls and for certain humanities and home economics subjects for boys in second-level schools.

Research into the guidance and counselling experiences of female and male students prior to making further education, training and career choices during post-primary education is required. Research is also required into the nature and extent of guidance received by students prior to and during their participation in Post-Leaving Certificate courses.

Gendered subject take-up in second level would suggest that young women and men are strongly predisposed to choose gender-stereotypical careers in further and higher education and there is ample evidence that this is happening (Clancy 1995; Clancy and Wall 2000; Galligan 2000). The gendered character of subject take-up is highly visible in the further education sector. Both females and males are concentrated in traditional gendered areas of training. Women are concentrated in the very high number of secretarial, business-based and child care courses provided; men are concentrated in more technical and industrial-type courses. In higher education, although women now constitute 55 per cent of science students, they make up over two-thirds (67 per cent) of arts and humanities students but only 19 per cent of engineering students (Galligan 2000: 61).

3.3 Diversity recognition issues

Promoting equality in education is not simply a matter of providing education services on equal terms to women and men. While it is essential to have equality of provision to have equality, it is also essential to create cultures in schools and in colleges that are equally welcoming of both genders (a principle that applies to all other groups named in the equality legislation). If the ethos of schools or colleges is such that one or other gender does not feel 'at home' or feels that they 'do not belong', then clearly this is not a gender-inclusive working or learning environment; it is not an environment in which equality can flourish. While organisational procedures are a core element in creating ethos, an important part of the gender-inclusive ethos is the curriculum itself. Not only must the culture of the organisation be gender inclusive, the subject material must also be gender inclusive.

Educators have long been concerned with the impact of coeducation on the learning experiences of female learners in terms of participation and attainment (Stanworth 1983; Weiner 1994; Younger and Warrington 1996). Studies of classroom interaction and participation demonstrate how in coeducational situations certain male learners (those with dominant interaction and learning styles) tend to dominate the public verbal space (Spender 1982; Morgan 1991; Tobin 1993; Lodge 1998; Drudy and Uí Chatháin 1999; Lynch and Lodge 2002). Thus, in coeducational learning environments, girls are less likely to be the visible or dominant group. Their relative invisibility extends outside the classroom, however, and finds expression in the lower status and recognition accorded to female-related extracurricular activities, including sporting activities. However, less dominant males may also experience invisibility and lower status (Lynch and Lodge 2002).

The reinforcement of gender stereotypes through both formal and informal sexist practices occurs for both male and female students. Yet this is by no means limited to coeducational institutions (Lynch 1989). Single-sex learning environments are also spaces where gender hierarchies and stereotypes can and do become exaggerated (Lynch and

Lodge 2002). The extent to which male principals are appointed in all-female schools with mostly female staff is an example of how gender hierarchies are reinforced in appointment procedures in single-sex schools (the reverse rarely happens). Uniform regulations based on traditional gender stereotypes and expectations are also an example of gender stereotyping. While issues regarding personal appearance and dress may appear to be relatively trivial to those outside of compulsory education, the fact is that these are experienced as significant equality concerns by many second-level students (Lynch and Lodge 2002). The recent recommendation by the Equality Officer (under the Employment Equality Act 1998) that CERT's requirement that female trainees wear skirts was discriminatory on the gender ground (Equality Authority 2001) has implications for educational and training institutions with gender-based uniform regulations, the majority of which are within the compulsory sector.

It is well recognised internationally that what counts as valued knowledge in much of formal education is strongly biased in gender terms (and indeed in terms of social class, ethnicity, etc.) (Smith 1987; Harding 1991). A further factor that militates against equality, therefore, is the gendered character of the knowledge and discourses within education itself. Although there has been no national study in Ireland of gender bias within the curricula and syllabi of our schools and colleges, even a cursory review of the curricula and syllabi suggests that it is the life and work of male writers, scientists, artists, historians, etc. that dominate the world of learning for most young women and men. Given the way in which domain assumptions[4] of all intellectuals influence how they interpret the world (Gouldner 1971) (and the consequent impact of biographical experience, social class, gender, ethnicity, etc. on their world view), it is clear that with male-produced scholarship dominating the world of learning, male biases are written into the texts that are studied and the subjects addressed. This is frequently a highly invisible process, however, as the male definition of the subject has often become synonymous with the subject itself (Smith 1987).

---

[4]Domain assumptions are those nontheoretical beliefs and assumptions that intellectuals hold which have been developed through biographical experience. They are sets of values and beliefs that develop from specific cultural, political, gender, religious or other experiences and predispose us to interpret and value phenomena in very different ways. They are separate from the 'paradigmatic assumptions' developed from the theoretical standpoints taken on particular issues (Gouldner 1971).

3.4 Harassment

Sexual and other forms of harassment have not been studied in any depth in Irish schools and colleges, thus it is difficult to assess the scope of the issues involved. However, the limited data available from other studies suggests that there is a need for systematic research on the subject of harassment. Warren and O'Connor (1999) found that gender-based joking by male colleagues acted as a deterrent to female teachers considering promotion. There is also evidence that sexist behaviour and attitudes are so much a part of the ethos of some schools that they actually go unnoticed (Lynch and Lodge 1999). The recent successful case on harassment taken on behalf of two female second-level teachers (who had been subjected to sexual harassment by male students) shows, however, that such harassment issues can be addressed (the Labour Court determination in this case was announced in January 2002 – Determination No. DEE021).

3.5 Employment equality issues

Teaching is becoming an increasingly feminised profession (Warren and O'Connor 1999). This is particularly true of the primary sector (Drudy and Lynch 1993). Despite this, women are seriously under-represented in management across all educational sectors (Lynch 1999). When schools are amalgamated, women are less likely to retain their position as principal than their male counterparts (Warren and O'Connor 1999). Where access to promotion is through open competition, women applicants are less likely to be successful than when promotions are based on seniority. Women are also under-represented in the third-level sector, particularly in management posts, senior lectureships and professorships, although this situation is by no means unique to Ireland (Neville 1996; Eurostat 2001). As Glendenning (1999) observes, there is a large body of case law demonstrating that gender has been used by schools in a discriminatory manner with regard to appointments, conditions of employment and promotion. The cases taken have mainly concerned discrimination against women.

All of this has serious implications for the appointments and promotional procedures in operation in schools and third-level institutions – it implies that the current systems in operation are disadvantaging women applicants. One obvious way in which the promotion and appointments systems are biased against women is through the biases built into appointments and promotions panels. Warren and O'Connor (1999: 84) report that a number of women in their study had been interviewed by male-only panels, an experience that led to them feeling 'dismayed and thrown off balance'.

Women's lack of representation at decision-making levels within education is not only confined to schools. It is mirrored by the situation in the Department of Education and Science and in the teacher unions, where senior posts are held disproportionately by men. The Equality Committee of the Irish National Teachers' Organization (INTO) is, for example, the only committee in that union which has a higher proportion of female than male participants (INTO 2001).

3.6 Good practice initiatives

• The Department of Education and Science established a Gender Equality Unit in 2001. The Unit advises on, reviews and promotes the development of policy. The aim is to support the Department of Education and Science's move to a gender-visible position in all areas of education.

• The Department of Education and Science has supported research into gender equality issues since the early 1980s, when it was one of the principal bodies initiating the study of gender issues in schools. Since that time it has financed or taken part in other research and intervention programmes across the range of educational sectors (Department of Education and Science 1998a). The studies and programmes targeted at primary schools include some mentioned above, such as *Equal Opportunities for Girls and Boys* and the *Gender Equity Action Research Project*. The Department has also issued material based on particular projects to primary teachers through their schools, including *Guidelines to Promote Gender Equality for Teachers*, which is an element of the *Equality Pack*. (The *Equality Pack* also contains an action research project and three other publications.) It has also developed a curriculum intervention project entitled *Technology/Science in the Primary School*.

• The Department of Education and Science has initiated a number of pilot projects at second level. Some of these have been focused on particular curricular areas. They include *Futures* (originally entitled *Girls into Technology*) and the *Intervention Project in Physics and Chemistry*. The Department has also supported the development of *Stars, Shells and Bluebells* by WITS, the Irish Association for Women in Technology and

Science. Other programmes, such as *Exploring Sex Stereotyping* and *'Balance'*, are more concerned with promoting awareness of gender issues within the context of social and personal development and management.

• Curriculum developments at both primary and post-primary level in recent years have included material focusing on personal and social development, particularly on education for citizenship. The Social, Political and Health Education (SPHE) and Civic, Social and Political Education (CSPE) curricula include components on gender equality issues, as does the Relationship and Sexuality Education (RSE) material. The *Exploring Masculinities* programme (Department of Education and Science 2000e) has been designed for use in single-sex boys' schools and is concerned with enabling boys to critically examine masculine identities and behaviour in order to foster balanced personal development. Guidelines on countering bullying include reference to issues relating to sexual harassment. The *Revised Primary School Curriculum* (Department of Education and Science 1999b) does not contain any of the gender-differentiated material that was evident in the so-called New Curriculum (Department of Education 1971).

• There are some welcome developments in preservice teacher education. Teachers in the Education Department, NUI Maynooth conduct a reflective project examining the verbal interactions taking place in one of their own classes. Those in coeducational settings specifically examine whether the class they analyse has fair and equal participation by female and male students. When writing up reports on their teaching practice for assessment, the students are required to identify examples of their own practice that impede the fair participation by female and male students. They are asked to make recommendations about ways in which they can change their future practice to ensure greater gender equality (Drudy and Uí Chatháin 1999).

• The Department of Education and Science has funded a number of research projects on second-level education examining gender equality issues, including *Coeducation and Gender Equality* (Hannan *et al.* 1996) and *Inside Classrooms: The Teaching and Learning of Mathematics in Social Context* (Lyons *et al.* 2003). In the 2003–04 academic year, the Department funded eighteen research projects and six doctoral nurseries on issues relating to gender equality.

- At third level, the Department of Education and Science has supported the *Introducing Technology* programme in the institutes of technology.

- The Department of Education and Science initiated a scheme to give funding support to women's adult education groups between 1997 and 1999. This was targeted in particular at women who are educationally disadvantaged. The scheme was operated in partnership with other agencies, including the Combat Poverty Agency, community education networks and adult education organisations. As McMinn (2000) points out, many women's community education programmes have been established in response to the poverty, social exclusion and isolation experienced by women in urban and rural communities around the country. These have provided their participants with affirmation and support, as well as providing personal development and other educational outcomes.

- In 1998 the Women's Education Initiative was established with assistance from the EU Community Support Framework. It offers support to education groups for women who are disadvantaged. This initiative has been replaced by the Education Equality Initiative, which is aided by the European Social Fund under the 2000–06 EU Community Support Framework. The projects selected for funding under this initiative are intended to develop models of good practice in tackling educational disadvantage among adults. This measure also targets men's education groups and mixed groups, including those with disabilities, members of the Traveller community and drug users.[5]

- The National Women's Council of Ireland initiated research in 1999 into six key areas of women's lives, including education. The *Millennium Project* reported on how women themselves envisaged the most suitable educational forms and supports that would meet their needs and respond to their lived experience (National Women's Council of Ireland 2001). This activity, which actively involves the target groups, the service providers and policy makers as equal participants, is a model of good emancipatory research practice in action.

---

[5]Information is available at www.education.ie/servlet/blobservlet/fe_guidelines_eei2.doc.

- The Equality Committee of the INTO[6] has made recommendations to the union to alter organisational practices in order to increase the participation of its women members, for example, ensuring that there is gender balance of members on union delegations. It has prepared studies on issues such as gender and educational leadership and workplace bullying. Gender equality issues have become an integrated part of all INTO documents, procedures and policies. The organisation has also promoted gender equality in schools through publications such as *Fair Play for Boys and Girls* and monitors the inclusion of a gender equality dimension into all its in-service courses.

- The ASTI lends its support to the promotion of equal opportunities for students, trade union members and teachers as employees. The ASTI circulated a model policy on gender equality for all Boards and devised guidelines for branch officers to promote equal opportunities for students across the nine grounds. It conducts an audit for its annual report each year detailing the gender profile of office holders within the union and in 2004 has commissioned research, funded by the Department of Education and Science, concerning promotional opportunities for females.

- The Teachers' Union of Ireland (TUI) has issued guidelines to its sixty-one branch officers with responsibility for equality. These guidelines state that the equality officers should actively encourage and monitor gender balance in branch activity, including branch representation in activities such as annual congress, training courses, conferences and TUI committees. Branch equality officers also seek to monitor gender equality in the employment of TUI members by encouraging women to apply for promotional posts and by seeking to monitor the composition of interview and selection boards. The Executive Committee of the TUI is charged with ensuring all of the union's policies and agreements are gender proofed.

---

[6]The ASTI's Equality Committee was originally focused on gender equality issues, but was renamed the Equal Opportunities Committee and is now focused on equality issues across the nine grounds named in the legislation (www.asti.ie). The TUI's Equality Officer is concerned with gender equality issues.

Chapter 4

Marital Status and Family Status

4.1 Introduction and background information

Marital status is defined in both the Employment Equality Acts and the Equal Status Acts as being 'single, married, separated, divorced or widowed'. Family status is defined as being a parent (or a person *in loco parentis*) for a child under eighteen years old, or as a parent or resident primary carer of a person eighteen years old or over who has a disability and who requires regular or frequent care. Family status as defined in the Equal Status Act also covers those who are pregnant.[7]

Given the overlap in the relevant issues, these two grounds are discussed together in this report. In addition, we mainly focus here on issues arising for young people in the formal education system, although issues facing adults returning to work are also briefly touched on.

4.2 Presence and participation issues

To date, the impact of marital status on access to, participation in or success in education has not been researched in Ireland in any systematic manner. Given the focus of most research on young people in education, the question of marital status has not typically arisen. The significance of family status for participation in education by young people may arise in relation to the impact of pregnancy and parenthood and in respect of other caring responsibilities.

---

[7]European law means that protection in an employment context for those who are pregnant is covered by the gender ground rather than the family status ground under the Employment Equality Act.

Pregnancy and parenthood

Between 1999 and 2002 a total of 7,235 births were registered among young women aged fifteen to eighteen years[8], an age at which young women are generally still at school. The number of children born to mothers aged nineteen, twenty and twenty-one, i.e. the typical age group of those who move into further and higher education directly after schooling, was 17,597.

We do not know how many of these young women become pregnant while they are still at school, although there is some evidence that early school leaving precedes pregnancy (Hannan and O'Riain 1993; McCashin 1996, 1997; Department of Social, Community and Family Affairs 2000). Neither do we know how many become pregnant while engaged in further or higher education. There is a further lack of research on the experiences of those young women who become pregnant while in education (at primary, post-primary or tertiary levels). Apart from the limited research evidence summarised below, we know very little regarding pregnancy, either as a reason for leaving education or as a reason for being excluded from participation in education.

The difficulties facing pregnant school children and students are considerable. Most immediately, at second level the schoolgirl often has to confront schools' reluctance to recognise that students who become pregnant may wish to stay in school and return after the birth of the baby (Murphy 2001).[9] Students who are pregnant may also be faced with deferral of examinations or courses. The Department of Education and Science does encourage young women to remain in education during pregnancy. On application, it provides for up to nine hours of home tuition for ten weeks for students who cannot attend school, including young women who are pregnant. Although some of this support can be availed of after the birth of the baby, it could be argued that the Department of Education and Science makes no ongoing provision for these young women after their baby is born. Writing a decade ago, Magee (1994) highlighted the difficulties facing young

---

[8]264 births were registered to mothers who were fifteen years old and under; 926 births to mothers aged sixteen; 2,062 births to mothers aged seventeen; and 3,983 births to mothers aged eighteen (Vital Statistics 2002).

[9]Some schools may be reluctant to accommodate visibly pregnant female students. In January 2003 a court in Northern Ireland found that a girls' post-primary school in Co. Fermanagh had discriminated against a female student when it did not allow her either to attend that school or to sit state examinations there once her pregnancy became visible.

women with children seeking to engage in education and training programmes arising out of the lack of affordable crèche or child care facilities.

At third level, pregnancy and birth may also cause students to defer summer examinations, which in turn may result in the student being deemed ineligible for honours resits. Although individual departments, colleges and schools can and do opt to be flexible in the application of these procedures, the absence of regulations is often a further source of anxiety for students who are pregnant.

Accommodating students who are pregnant means taking account of factors like their need to attend prenatal classes, their inability to carry heavy school bags and their need for suitable clothing and seating, especially in the latter stages of pregnancy. Yet there are no national guidelines or support systems for assisting schools on most of these policy matters.[10] Among the issues that need to be addressed, therefore, are the lack of specialised guidance and counselling programmes and support services, the lack of teacher education about pregnancy and parenting among school children and the absence of a national policy and funding in relation to pregnancy in schools and colleges (NESF 2001: 67).

While the issues involved will vary depending on particular family circumstances, young parents face considerable obstacles to remaining in education. Child care is an obvious obstacle facing all young parents, perhaps particularly for students who are away from home. Because many third-level colleges do not have crèches on site, child care frequently has to be accessed on the private market at a cost that is prohibitive for the student even if it is subvented. Students attending colleges away from home also experience difficulties in finding suitable, reasonably priced accommodation if they have a child.

Richardson (2000) has reported that young women who are lone parents are more likely to have a low level of educational attainment and to leave school early. Lone mothers, especially those on the One-Parent Family Payment, are among the most educationally disadvantaged lone parents generally and face considerable difficulties in returning to

---

[10]In 2000 the Department of Education and Science issued posters, information leaflets and the report of a working group to schools that highlighted the potential health hazard of heavy school bags and outlined some measures that schools could take to alleviate the problem. Although these measures did not have pregnant students specifically in mind, they would be of benefit to them.

education. This issue has been recognised in financial supports for single parents returning to education.

Recipients of the One-Parent Family Payment who are between eighteen and twenty years of age, who have been on that allowance for a minimum of six months and who have been out of education for two years are eligible for the Back to Education Allowance to enable them to attend full-time second-level courses. Those aged twenty-one or over do not need to have been out of education for two years and are not restricted to second-level courses. The Back to Education Allowance is paid at the same rate as the One-Parent Family Payment and also provides a 'cost of education allowance' at the start of each academic year. Secondary benefits, such as rent supplement and a medical card, can also be retained.

Despite its availability, the number of One-Parent Family Payment recipients availing of the Back to Education Allowance is quite small (636), with most of those attending third-level courses (Department of Social, Community and Family Affairs 2000). The *Review of the One-Parent Family Payment* suggests that there are a number of reasons for this. Many lone parents are early school leavers who are too young to avail of this allowance. In addition, the courses offered frequently do not suit the needs of lone parents, as they are longer than the school day for primary school children and there is no supporting child care provision.

Other caring responsibilities

It is important to recognise that young people may have caring responsibilities other than as parents.[11] The term 'carers' is associated with adults and in its strictest legal sense may suggest full-time responsibilities. Other forms of care duty may not meet the formal legal definition but are still relevant. While adult women undertake most care work, carers are not a homogenous group in terms of age and marital status. Duties of caring for dependent family members fall not only on adults but also sometimes on children, teenagers and young adults. This can be the result of particular family circumstances, such as the death of a parent, acute or chronic parental illness, parental separation or the demands of parents' working hours. There is no available data on this

[11]Care work in Ireland, be it the care of children, those who are ill, older people or people with disabilities in need of care, is predominantly undertaken by women, although the number of men involved has increased in recent years (Commission on the Family 1998).

group of young people and the impact of their care work on their educational opportunities and these issues are touched on only marginally in existing research.

Young people in schools are involved in a range of domestic labour activity, including caring work and part-time work (Hannan *et al.* 1996; APVSCC 1998; Lodge and Lynch 2000). In a national survey conducted by the Association of Principals of Vocational Schools and Community Colleges (APVSCC), almost one-fifth (18 per cent) of all participants were identified as being at risk of consistent absenteeism. Almost one-third (31 per cent) of the respondents gave work or helping at home as their second reason for frequent absence from school. At primary level, the INTO (1995) identified a variety of reasons for absenteeism, which included home-related factors. The INTO notes particular difficulties in a very small number of cases where drug- or alcohol-dependent parents keep children at home from school to either care for younger siblings or for the parent himself or herself.

School attendance among young teenage Travellers is low, with approximately one-fifth of all Traveller young people aged between twelve and fifteen not receiving any formal education (Bourke 1998). While the reasons for this are complex, there is a strong tradition within Traveller culture of young people assuming adult responsibilities at a relatively early age. Many Traveller girls and young women take on caring roles within their own families while they are still of school-going age (Trainees of St Joseph's Training Centre 2000).

Responsibility for care work can be a ground on which people can be indirectly or directly excluded from education. Schools can experience difficulties in meeting the needs of the minority of students on their rolls who have family caring responsibilities and may need a greater level of flexibility with regard to attendance. However, as we have seen, these issues have not received any in-depth examination to date and there is a need for much more research on the interface between care work and educational exclusion.

Marital and family status can also be important factors for adults returning to education. One way in which marital status has a direct impact, particularly on access to further and higher education, is through the grant procedures. In this case, it is dependent married persons (most of whom are women) who are indirectly disadvantaged. Support for third-level mature students is means tested, the means assessed being those of the applicant and/or that of their spouse if he or she is married. Dependency is therefore a core assumption of the grant procedure. In 2003 the household income of a family with fewer than four dependents had to be less than €32,000 for a full grant, i.e. registration fee refund and full maintenance, totalling €2,885, where there are four or fewer dependent persons. What this means in practice is that the eligibility of a married person without an income for a grant is assessed on the basis of their partner's income (Department of Education and Science 2002a, 2002c). Their partner, if he or she so wishes, may prevent them from entering higher education if he or she refuses to pay the fees or maintenance and they have no independent means. Because education support is based on a principle of assumed dependency and not on the principle of individual rights to education (as it is in Germany), those who are dependent on a spouse (and these are mostly women) cannot return to higher education without their partner's support if the spouse's income exceeds the defined limits. This is an issue not only for married people who are dependent, but also for people who are dependent on their parents, as the same principles apply in their case. There is a need for research on the issue of participation in further and higher education among those who are economically dependent on others, as little is known about it currently.

Adults who are caring for children or for a dependent adult relative also experience difficulties in accessing education in the noncompulsory sector (third-level, training and further education). Child care is expensive and there is limited relief care for those with responsibility for dependent adults. The timing of education programmes that are full time or whole day also creates difficulties for adults with caring responsibilities. The care involved either in the rearing of young children or in looking after a dependent adult relative is ongoing. The primary carer of any dependent person cannot go to their local educational provider, even for a few hours a day, to pursue any kind of course or training unless there is someone else available to take over their caring role during that time. Child care costs in Ireland are among the highest in the European Union, exceeded only by Greece and the UK (Goodbody Economic Consultants 1998). Unless there is a comprehensive child care policy, and indeed a comprehensive policy meeting the needs of those caring for adult dependent relatives, other measures to encourage greater participation in education cannot but be severely constrained (Ryan 1997, cited in Richardson 2000).

4.3 Diversity recognition issues

There are subtle ways in which people with different marital or family statuses may be accorded lack of recognition in education, especially in images, stories and other systems of representation. Being single, for example, is certainly not presented as a norm in education programmes, including those dealing with relationships. Byrne (1997) suggests that the single state has been denigrated, especially for women. Yet a sizeable minority of Irish adults remain single, and this has been so for long periods of history (Kennedy 1973; Byrne 1997).

Textbooks and syllabus material have also been found to display traditional biases in terms of marital and family status. Nuclear family units (two parents and dependent children) have tended to predominate in curricular materials used in primary schools. This is especially true of the content and illustrations of reading books, language lessons and materials such as those used in religious education programmes. The nuclear family has tended to be regarded as the normal or average family. Not only does this render invisible the one-parent family unit, but it also means that families consisting only of adults are excluded.

There is a need to examine curricular materials used in both primary and post-primary schools, therefore, to ensure that parity of esteem is afforded to those who are divorced, separated, widowed and single as well as those who are married. There is also a need for education programmes concerned with relationships, health and sexuality not to pathologise particular marital or family statuses.

Of obvious relevance here are negative perceptions regarding one-parent families as a family unit (Commission on the Family 1998). Lone-parent households constituted 11 per cent of households in 1996 and an estimated 13 per cent currently; 82 per cent of lone parents are women (NESF 2001: 20–1). Most lone parents with one child under fifteen are separated or divorced (51 per cent) and 12 per cent are widowed; single parents generally (that is to say, parents who were never married) remain a minority among lone parents (37 per cent) (Fahey *et al.* 1998: 196). Lone parents are a heterogeneous group with differences in age, family life cycle, marital status, sexual orientation, economic status and gender (McCashin 1993; Department of Social, Community and Family Affairs 2000; Richardson 2000).

A large-scale study of social prejudice in Ireland found that just under half of all those surveyed believed that a single mother could not raise a child as effectively as a married couple, with attitudes towards the parenting ability of a single father being noticeably more negative (MacGreil 1996). Such attitudes can mean that those who belong to family units that do not fit the traditional norm can experience a failure on the part of educational institutions to provide the conditions necessary to enable full participation.

Some individuals may experience rejection or lack of recognition because of their different family status. They may be made to feel unwelcome, humiliated and excluded. Interviews with teachers during the course of a study of primary schools revealed a high level of teacher awareness of different children's family circumstances. Some teachers and other school-related personnel tended to use membership of a lone-parent household as an explanation for students' poor academic attainment and behaviour (Lodge 1998). However, teacher education, at either preservice or in-service stages, has not provided systematic programmes to counteract such prejudices.

At second level, curricular material that focuses on the life of the family is less visible. The material in the previous Home Economics syllabus (which was phased out in 2002) presented the family as a social institution in a manner that failed to grant equal esteem to one-parent families. The syllabus suggested that one-parent families could be 'problem families' experiencing poverty, isolation and emotional difficulties and lacking role models for children (Department of Education 1969). The reasons for the poverty or isolation, etc. were not examined. The revised Home Economics syllabus (Department of Education and Science 2001) includes a broader understanding of family, reflecting the changing nature and greater diversity of Irish society. However, a change of syllabus content will not in and of itself necessarily bring about change in either the attitudes or pedagogical approaches of those who teach the syllabus.

The fact that school children themselves may leave second-level school with no education about child care and its demands must also be identified as a factor that exacerbates the difficulties of young mothers and fathers. While there are relationship and sexuality education courses and health and education programmes in schools, these programmes have not been implemented systematically across all schools, as in the past schools had quite a high level of discretion in their implementation.[12] The net

---

[12]All schools are required to cover the complete RSE syllabus from the 2003–04 school year on.

effect of this policy was that some young people have left compulsory education in Ireland with a minimal level of education in relation to sexuality and relationships and may have a limited understanding of the nature of caring as a life task.

4.4 Employment equality issues

All female employees in the state have a statutory right to maternity leave and protection of their employment while on such leave. Those who are permanent teachers in primary or post-primary institutions do not experience problems in availing of their statutory rights, and the Department of Education and Science normally makes provision for a substitute teacher. The situation for women working in third-level institutions is more problematic, especially if they are academics. As Keher (1996) points out, the maternity leave legislation does not provide for cover substitution. As a consequence, women academics who are pregnant do not always take up their statutory rights. They can organise and pay their own substitute and they can also arrange their teaching workload so that additional teaching is done prior to and following their absence for maternity leave. Some continue to do departmental work during their period of leave. Some women academics reported negative reactions to their taking of maternity leave by male colleagues and expressed concerns regarding promotional prospects (Keher 1996).

As is outlined in Chapter 3 on gender, there are quite significant differences in the promotion and appointment patterns of women and men to middle or senior management positions at all levels of education (Lynch 1994; Egan 1996; Warren and O'Connor 1999). While some of this is accounted for by different application rates, this does not fully account for the difference. There are a host of factors at play, some of which are related to marital status. A study conducted on behalf of the Teachers' Union of Ireland (TUI) reported that both female and male teachers believed that being married was a disadvantage for a woman teacher seeking promotion (Teachers' Union of Ireland 1990). Not all instances of discrimination due to marital status involve women, however. Nor are such cases always concerned with the fact that the complainant is married. Glendenning (1999: 402) describes a case in which a single male successfully took a case against his educational employer because he suffered discrimination as a result of being single.

A further equality issue arising in relation to marital status concerns the impact of a teacher's lifestyle on his or her employment rights.

Glendenning (1999) suggests that the conflicting rights of employers and employees are most manifest with regard to the potential clash between the individual lifestyle of a teacher and the ethos of the school where he or she is employed. In 1985 the Employment Appeals Tribunal upheld the right of a school to dismiss a teacher because her relationship with a married man contravened the norms and values promoted by the school (ibid.). As a consequence of the High Court decision on the case and the subsequent exemptions in the Employment Equality Acts relating to certain types of institution with a religious ethos, teachers (and others) have expressed concern at the possibility that an employee might be dismissed from a denominationally owned school because they have an 'inappropriate' lifestyle, namely one that is defined as being not in accord with the school's ethos (Mullally 2001).

4.5 Good practice initiatives

- The Waterford Student Mothers Support Group is an initiative by the Waterford Area Partnership and the Home–School Liaison Co-ordinator. This is a programme to support secondary school students while pregnant and in early motherhood. Support and guidance are provided at both the group and individual levels. The programme helped all twelve students to remain in school. The programme is now supported by the Department of Education and Science and was cited in the National Economic and Social Forum's *Lone Parents* report (NESF 2001) as a model of good practice and the type of initiative that should be mainstreamed.

- The *Review of the One-Parent Family Payment* carried out by the Department of Social, Community and Family Affairs (2000) identified a number of projects specifically aimed at lone parents or incorporating some element of work with lone parents. Among those noted were the Moving On project, which supports young mothers into training, education and employment. The Teenage Health Initiative targets adolescents at risk of pregnancy through a positive education programme. Other projects identified include Family Services projects; teenage parenting support projects; the SpringBoard initiative; Community Mothers Scheme; Family Resource Project; Neighbourhood Youth Projects; Family Support Workers; community child care workers; parenting programmes; preschool services and after-school services; and Relationships and Sexuality Education.

- Foróige, the national youth development organisation, and the National Youth Federation have introduced a number of initiatives. One of these, the Young Mothers Groups project,[13] involves the young women themselves in planning, implementing and evaluating the programme.

- As noted in the introduction, there is some evidence that in a small number of cases young people's caring responsibilities within their families have a negative impact on their education. The National Educational Welfare Board, which established under the Education (Welfare) Act 2000, has responsibility for co-ordinating and implementing policies relating to attendance and other related educational welfare issues. It will target all problem areas and groups rather than focusing on specific large urban areas.

- Child care or relief care (for dependants other than children) is an essential service to enable individuals who are primary carers to participate in education. The availability of crèche facilities at some VTOS courses, for example, makes those centres more accessible to those caring for young children. The limited number of crèche places available in third-level institutions is also a useful support for those students who can access them.

---

[13]There are seven such groups in Dublin and one in Cork.

Chapter 5
Sexual Orientation

5.1 Introduction and background information
Sexual orientation is defined in the equality legislation to mean heterosexual, homosexual or bisexual orientation.

The discussion of equality concerns under this ground focuses mainly on second-level schools and to a lesser extent comments on aspects of other levels of educational provision. There are two reasons for this. First, much of the very limited research that has been conducted is focused on adolescents and their experiences of education. Second, as O'Carroll and Szalacha (2000) argue, self-realisation by individuals of their sexual identities takes place during and is a core process of adolescence. During this time, the majority of young people are students of second-level schools. The issue of equality in education for lesbian, gay and bisexual people was addressed by the Equality Authority in its report *Implementing Equality for Lesbians, Gays and Bisexuals* (Equality Authority 2002a).

5.2 Presence and participation issues
There is no example from the limited Irish research on sexual orientation and education of overt denial of admission of a student to a learning institution or of denial of access to any courses or other facilities on the ground of sexual orientation. Equally, there is no recorded evidence of any student being overtly prevented from participating in education because of their sexual orientation. Nevertheless, the limited research on gay or lesbian young people's experiences of education is not encouraging – it identifies isolation, depression and loneliness among students because of their sexual orientation. These experiences are coupled with a fear of being known to be different, regarded as deviant or living in fear of being rejected or beaten (GLEN/Nexus 1995).

Lesbian, gay and bisexual youth are at risk of experiencing social isolation, rejection by family and peers, violence, harassment, school dropout, running away and depression as a consequence of negative reactions to their sexual orientation (Stevens and Morgan 1999). This lack of recognition of different sexual orientations in school reflects a wider social isolation and rejection of those who are not heterosexual (Moane 1995).

Approximately 60 per cent of the participants in a study on poverty and lesbians and gay men reported negative experiences of their second-level education (GLEN/Nexus 1995). These included isolation and loneliness resulting in depression, severe self-criticism and low self-esteem. These negative feelings were attributed almost totally to their sexual orientation. One of the consequences of the resulting stress was poor academic achievement – 40 per cent of those reporting difficulties or negative experiences of school found their school work hard to cope with. A small number of participants attributed their early school leaving to the stress they felt in coping with their sexual orientation while in school.

Participants in the GLEN/Nexus study (1995) who went to college reported difficulties similar to the ones encountered at second level. Again, isolation and loneliness, coupled with fear of rejection or harassment, led to stress, low self-esteem and difficulties coping with the academic workload. A small number of these dropped out of college as a result of the stress they experienced. Almost half of the participants in this study had taken part in a training course (including some of those who had attended third-level institutions). As in other sectors, over half of the training participants reported problems such as isolation, depression and stress that they attributed to their sexual orientation and the lack of institutional acceptance of difference. A small number dropped out of their training course as a result of the stress experienced, while others considered that their workload was difficult to cope with as a result of the isolation and stress they suffered (GLEN/Nexus 1995).

5.3 Diversity recognition issues

For some groups, the fact that significant aspects of their lives and experiences are rendered invisible and completely overlooked serves to oppress them (Young 1990). It is oppression through invisibility that best encapsulates the educational experiences of gay, lesbian or bisexual students, and indeed teachers, in Ireland (Rose 1994; GLEN/Nexus 1995; Barron 1999; Foyle Friend 1999; Gay HIV Strategies & Nexus 1999; Gowran 2000; O'Carroll and Szalacha 2000). It is not surprising, therefore, that very little Irish research has been conducted in this area at any level of education. The absence of research into the heterosexist nature of education shows in turn just how invisible the issue of difference in sexual orientations is in schools. The lack of any baseline research also makes it difficult to systematically explore the equality issues that arise for students or teachers who are gay, lesbian or bisexual. Where gay, lesbian or bisexual experience is recognised at all within education provision, particularly at primary or second level, it is pathologised and labelled deviant (Gowran 2000). Often when words such as 'gay' or 'lesbian' (or slang equivalents of such words) are heard in an educational context, they are used as terms of derision or abuse (Lynch and Lodge 1999; Wallace 2001).

Silence around sexual orientation extends into the formal curriculum. Teaching on sexuality takes place in Irish schools (at both primary and second level) within the context of Social, Personal and Health Education (SPHE). This is an area in which gay, lesbian and bisexual identity might be expected to be visible. However, much of this programme is premised on assumptions of heterosexuality. Indeed, as O'Carroll and Szalacha (2000) argue, the topic of sexual orientation had been ignored within the Relationships and Sexuality Education (RSE) programme. They note that during the course of their research, it emerged that not a single second-level school had completed the sexual orientation component of the RSE programme. However, schools have been obliged to cover the complete RSE programme since the 2003–04 school year.

Almost all of the published material from the SPHE primary curriculum or junior cycle syllabus is characterised by an assumption of heterosexuality as well as an emphasis on the procreative nature of sexuality. For example, in the fifth and sixth class guidelines for SPHE, the section on 'Birth and New Life' recommends that the pupils should be enabled to 'understand sexual intercourse, conception and birth within the context of a committed, loving relationship' (Department of Education and Science 1999a: 58). Furthermore, in the section for the same age group on friendship, there is a substantive difference made between the types of friendships that can occur between people of the same sex and the friendships between females and males, again with an assumption of universal heterosexuality.

At second level, the Relationships and Sexuality syllabus (within SPHE, Year 3) reiterates the assumed difference between same-sex friendships and those involving females and males and does not address gay or lesbian relationships. The junior cycle SPHE teacher guidelines discuss sexual attraction and falling in love in the context of young people's increased opportunity for socialising with the opposite sex and the establishment of heterosexual relationships (National Council for Curriculum and Assessment 2001). For those young people who are lesbian, gay or bisexual, the resulting silence and denial of their sexuality deprives them of an important aspect of their identity (Watney 1991).

The guidelines for both primary and second-level schools regarding the contents of programmes of education on sexuality and relationships stress the need for the specific curriculum to be prepared in consultation with parents, teachers and school management (Department of Education and Science 1999a, 2000b). While there is no doubt that any programme of personal development education is best delivered in partnership between school and home, the attitudes of individual parents (and indeed teachers) regarding controversial issues such as homosexuality may have resulted in the exclusion of these topics from the programmes of individual schools in the past. The denominational nature and resulting ethos of a large proportion of schools at both primary and second level may also have affected the type of contents deemed to be appropriate and how the material was taught. An evaluation of the RSE programme noted that approximately one-fifth of all primary teachers and almost one-third of all post-primary teachers surveyed perceived the vigorous objections by some people against the programme to be an obstacle to its implementation (Morgan 2000). The same report found that one-quarter of all primary and post-primary teachers surveyed believed that RSE was regarded as inappropriate by parents. However, as noted above, from the 2003–04 school year on, all schools are obliged to cover the syllabus.

The *Exploring Masculinities* programme for senior cycle boys in single-sex boys' schools includes a section exploring sexual orientation. Included among the objectives for this section are that students may:

- promote greater understanding and tolerance of people who have a bisexual, homosexual or lesbian orientation

- have a greater appreciation of the difficulties facing young men who wish to confide in their friends that they are gay (Department of Education and Science 2000e: 222).

The silence that surrounds sexual orientation in the education sector is reflective of a discomfort around sexual issues in general that has characterised Irish society over a lengthy period (Inglis 1999). It can be at least partly attributed to the dominance of Roman Catholic teaching and ideology in Irish society on matters of sexuality in general (Inglis 1998; Gowran 2000). It must be noted, however, that most major religions do not hold same-sex relationships in high regard. Deignan (2000) argues that Roman Catholic understanding of and teaching about sexuality is premised on its sole procreative purpose. Homosexuality is interpreted within such a frame as deviant and disordered in theological terms (Dillon 1999).

The silence around sexual orientation is also related to the way particular education stakeholders have dominated the debate around relationships and sexuality education. There was no input included in the RSE programme from potential stakeholders, such as gay and lesbian organisations or the organisation Parents' Support (O'Carroll and Szalacha 2000). Denominational interests as well as those of parent associations took priority. Due to the nature of the denominational management of the vast majority of Irish primary schools and a sizeable proportion of those at second level (Drudy and Lynch 1993), religious perspectives on homosexuality have had a significant impact on the material deemed appropriate. It is true that the Roman Catholic Church's attempt to ensure that sexuality education took place only within religion class failed. However, the programme's content for each school is negotiable with parents, teachers and management and must reflect the school's (denominational) ethos (Inglis 1998). Commentary or material produced by denominational bodies regarding appropriate content, resources and approaches for relationships and sexuality education reflect the different denominational perspectives (Fearon 1996; Coyle 1997). Neither the Roman Catholic Church nor most of the Protestant churches regard same-sex relationships as acceptable.

There are questions to be resolved, therefore, regarding the balancing of minority group rights, parental rights, students' rights to a sound education and the interests of powerful stakeholders within education who may be neither parent nor student.

5.4 Harassment

One of the key reasons given by the participants in the study by GLEN/Nexus (1995) for their negative experiences of education was fear of bullying or harassment should their sexual orientation become known. Some of the respondents described experiences of bullying, harassment, mockery and a sense of having been rejected by both peers and teachers at second level. A small number of those who had attended college also reported harassment or bullying. Recent research suggests that negative and intolerant attitudes towards people who are gay or lesbian are not just an historical phenomenon. Recent research shows that cultural norms of single-sex boys' schools in particular were hostile to those who were or could be suspected of being gay (Lodge and Lynch 2001; Lynch and Lodge 2002). The attitudes expressed by the young people (both sexes generally) are reflective of a wider social intolerance and homophobia (MacGreil 1996).

There is little formal recognition in an educational context of peer bullying because of sexual orientation. School guidelines on bullying issued by the Department of Education (1993) make limited reference to sexual orientation as a reason for bullying in schools. Interestingly, the Department's guidelines on dealing with bullying note that the role of the school in preventing such behaviour is crucial. The issue was also identified in reports by the Equality Authority (2002a) and the National Economic and Social Forum (NESF 2003). The fact that students can be bullied because they are gay, lesbian or bisexual (or assumed to be so) needs to be formally acknowledged in schools, especially given the silence that surrounds sexual orientation. Where schools allow a culture to develop that ignores bullying based on known or assumed sexual orientation, it can be argued that they are failing to provide a safe place of learning for their students (O'Carroll and Szalacha 2000).

When young people experience difficulties in educational institutions (whether these were schools, colleges or places of training), they report a marked reluctance to seek help or support from teachers, tutors or trainers (GLEN/Nexus 1995). The main source of support for those in third-level institutions was not the support services of the college itself; rather, students were more likely to use the services of the students' union or student societies (Union of Students in Ireland 2004). There is evidence that teachers and other educational professionals have lacked the kind of training that would sensitise them to the issues that can confront learners of all ages who are gay, lesbian or bisexual (GLEN/Nexus 1995), although the Department of Education and Science has provided training in RSE, including in relation to sexual orientation, since 1996.

5.5 Employment equality issues
The testimony of gay and lesbian teachers indicates that they have to engage in careful management of their sexual identity. This generates stress within a school context, especially a fear of being deprived of

employment should one's sexual orientation become known. Schools are not considered 'safe' places in which to be lesbian or gay (Gowran 2000).

There has been no major study in Ireland of the experiences of teachers who are gay, lesbian or bisexual. A small study (Gowran 2000) does suggest that working in schools is difficult for people who are not heterosexual. The teachers interviewed expressed fears about their private lives becoming publicly known within their schools. Some of the teachers feared they would lose their teaching jobs if it became known they had a same-sex partner; others had decided against pursuing promotions so as to guard their privacy about their sexuality. One participant claimed she had been discriminated against in relation to an appointment in another school because of her sexual orientation. The GLEN/Nexus study (1995) also reported that people who were gay, lesbian or bisexual decided against seeking teaching posts because of fears of discrimination and job loss.

The courts have recognised the rights of denominational institutions to protect their ethos, and in a case regarding the private life of an individual teacher during the 1980s upheld the right of a school not to employ someone whose lifestyle was contrary to the institution's values (Glendenning 1999). Teachers employed by denominational schools can therefore feel that they are expected to have values and lifestyles appropriate to the ethos of the school. Those who are gay, lesbian or bisexual are fearful of their identity becoming public precisely because their lifestyles may be interpreted by some as contradictory to the values of the school (Gowran 2000). Although the focus of much attention is on denominational schools, prejudice against lesbian, gay and bisexual people is by no means limited to those employed in denominational schools. In a study of the social climate of post-primary schools, one of the teachers claimed that she failed to acquire a permanent position in a nondenominational school because her lesbian identity was publicly known (Lynch and Lodge 2002).

5.6 Good practice initiatives

- O'Carroll and Szalacha (2000) have observed that there are few examples of good practice in second-levels schools in relation to education about sexual orientation. While there are schools where differences in sexual orientation are addressed, this is by no means a high-profile or core part of the education programme (Lynch and Lodge 2002).

- O'Carroll and Szalacha (2000) did outline a positive school programme on sexuality in operation in the United States, the Safe Schools Program. The purpose of this programme is to provide a harassment-free, positive environment for students who are gay, lesbian or bisexual. It involves the training of volunteer teachers and the active involvement of students in the establishment and running of a programme within their school. The teachers and students are focused on raising awareness and forming gay–straight alliances. Parent involvement has also formed an important part of the programme's success, as it enabled the school to broaden its focus to encompass identities that are outside of the traditional family context. The programme is not only focused on the proactive prevention of harassment and bullying of students based on their sexual orientation, but also has a broader remit. It aims to make visible the contributions and realities of the lives of those who are gay and lesbian in the life of the school and in the general curriculum.

- In an Irish context, the section on sexual orientation in the *Exploring Masculinities* senior cycle second-level programme sensitively tackles the complex issues involved in relation to sexual differences. It allows students space to consider a variety of perspectives and experiences and looks at the impact of isolation and harassment on those who are not accepted by peers. However, this programme is not compulsory in schools and was designed only for single-sex boys' schools.

- The Union of Students in Ireland (USI) has also taken a proactive role in tackling the invisibility of gay, lesbian and bisexual experiences. Challenging homophobia and consequent harassment in relation to it is one of USI's equality policies. It engages in awareness raising in its constituent colleges. USI has also actively supported the establishment of gay and lesbian societies in third-level institutions in Ireland.

Chapter 6
Religious Belief

6.1 Introduction and background information

Discrimination on the religion ground under the equality legislation occurs when one person is treated in a comparable situation less favourably than another person because they have a different religious belief, or because one has a religious belief and the other person does not. The term 'religious belief' includes religious background or outlook. Some of the particular provisions and exemptions that apply to the religion ground to be found in the Employment Equality Acts and the Equal Status Acts, respectively, are given in Tables 5 and 6.

Table 5. Some provisions in the Employment Equality Acts relating to the religion ground

---

Exemptions include
Certain religious, educational and medical institutions may give more favourable treatment on the religion ground to an employee or prospective employee where it is reasonable to do so in order to maintain the religious ethos of the institution.

Certain religious, educational and medical institutions may take action which is reasonably necessary to prevent an employee or a prospective employee from undermining the religious ethos of the institution.

Certain religious, educational and medical institutions may reserve places on specified vocational training courses and schools of nursing in such numbers (as seem necessary to the relevant Minister) to ensure the availability of nurses and primary teachers.

Table 6. Some provisions in the Equal Status Acts relating to the religion ground

---

Exemptions include

Primary and post-primary schools that have the objective of providing education in an environment which promotes certain religious values may admit persons of a particular religious denomination in preference to others and may refuse to admit a student who is not of that denomination if it is proved that the refusal is essential to maintain the ethos of the school.

Institutions established for providing training to ministers of a particular religion may admit students of only one religious belief.

While the great majority of the Irish population is Roman Catholic (Inglis 1998; Tovey and Share 2000), there has long been a minority population belonging to the various Protestant denominations (White 1975; Bowen 1983; Caird 1985; Murphy and Adair 2002). Ireland has also had a small Jewish community for over a century (Keogh 1997) and there has been a small but growing Islamic community in recent years. Other small groups of believers include members of the Baha'i community, Hindus, Sikhs, Buddhists, adherents of the Greek and Russian Orthodox churches and those with secular beliefs. Table 7 presents a breakdown for 1991 and 2002. The number of people who are Roman Catholic rose in absolute terms by approximately a quarter of a million over this period, but as a proportion of the total population it fell from 91.6 per cent of the population to 88.4 per cent. The percentage decrease is accounted for by the increase in the proportion of those who are of other religions and of no religion.

There are a number of ways in which religion differs from most of the other grounds in this book. The equality legislation makes specific provisions for certain institutions with a religious ethos, including schools, and religious institutions have played a major role in the provision of education in Ireland. This section, therefore, focuses more on the structures in education and less on the experience of education for individuals than other sections do.

Funding and control of education institutions
The compulsory sectors of Irish education are characterised by a high degree of denominational control and ownership. A number of judicial rulings have interpreted the 1937 Constitution as offering implied

Table 7. Population by religious grouping, 1991 and 2002

Religion	Population (000s)		Actual change
	1991	*2002*	*1991–2002*
Roman Catholic	3228.3	3462.6	234.3
Church of Ireland (including Protestant)	89.2	115.6	26.4
Christian (unspecified)	16.3	21.4	5.1
Presbyterian	13.2	20.6	7.4
Muslim (Islamic)	3.9	19.1	15.3
Orthodox	0.4	10.4	10.1
Methodist	5.0	10.0	5.0
Other stated religions	19.8	40.0	20.3
No religion	66.3	138.3	72.0
Not stated	83.4	79.1	–4.3
Total	3525.7	3917.2	391.5

Source: Census 2002: Principal Demographic Results

protection for the denominational nature of schooling (Glendenning 1999). Primary schools are almost entirely denominational, although there is a small but growing multidenominational sector, and most of the schools in this sector are in large urban centres. Over half (57 per cent) of all second-level schools are denominational, free-scheme or fee-paying, privately owned institutions. The great majority of secondary schools are Roman Catholic in ownership and control, with most of the remainder being under Protestant management. Vocational schools and community colleges are now formally defined as multidenominational second-level schools, although in practice many have been Roman Catholic in ethos in the past, given the predominantly Roman Catholic nature of their intake. While community schools are officially described as interdenominational, the terms of the deeds of trust mean that denominational bodies form part of their management structure (Drudy and Lynch 1993). All comprehensive schools are denominationally managed.

During the late 1960s, with the advent of the free secondary education scheme, a financial arrangement was made between the Department of Education and the Secondary Education Committee representing the four Protestant churches in the Republic. A block grant was made available to the educational authorities of the Protestant tradition to enable parents to send their children to denominationally appropriate secondary schools, many of which took boarders. The grant is paid directly to the school in question to cover fees or part of the fees. Families are means tested to ensure allocation of the monies according to need (Secondary Education Committee Grants Section 1999). While the block grant might appear to discriminate in favour of a particular religious belief, Glendenning (1999) argues that it operates to support parents' constitutional right to choose denominationally appropriate schools for their children. The means-tested provision of the block grant has enabled some young people of minority beliefs to attend a denominational secondary school that they could not afford to attend if they were dependent on personal resources. It goes some way towards recognising that Protestant religious minorities are a socio-economically diverse group.

The support given to Protestant families experiencing poverty to educate their children in schools within their own tradition is not a privilege that is given to other materially disadvantaged minorities, however. For example, many of the refugees, asylum seekers and other foreign nationals living in Ireland are not Roman Catholic, and in many cases are non-Christian. Many of these people are also socio-economically disadvantaged. However, the provision of financial assistance like the block grant to facilitate school choice has not been extended to such groups. In the case of asylum seekers the opposite is the case for those on direct provision; they have no means to send their children to schools that might be in accord with their religious beliefs (Fanning *et al.* 2001).

During the 1970s a number of attempts were made to establish multidenominational primary schools (Hyland 1996; Steer 1996; Cooke 1997). Some met with success (Hyland 1989; Griffin 1997) while others were unable to overcome the resistance of powerful interest groups, including the main churches and government Ministers (Cooke 1997). Such schools were traditionally at a financial disadvantage because they lacked a parish base and had great difficult raising the supplementary funds required at local level to start a new school. Since the late 1990s funding requirements for the establishment of these schools (and indeed for all new primary schools) have become somewhat less daunting with the introduction of a cap on the total local contribution.[14] Multidenominational national schools account for less than 1 per cent of all primary schools in the country. There is still no alternative to denominational education for a large number of parents and their children, especially for those who live outside the small number of urban centres where most multidenominational schools are located.

The Jewish and Islamic communities in Ireland operate one and two schools, respectively, for children of their own belief, all of which are in Dublin. None of the other minority religions have state-supported schools. Children from these latter communities, including those who hold secular beliefs (and indeed members of the Islamic or Jewish communities living at a distance from the relevant schools connected with their faith) are frequently obliged to attend whatever local school (primary or second level) grants them admission, regardless of its religious affiliation.

The only third-level institutions of a denominational nature are primary teacher education colleges (Tovey and Share 2000), institutions involved in the education of second-level teachers of religion and certain denominationally controlled hospitals where nurses are trained (Glendenning 1999).

6.2 Presence and participation issues

There is a dearth of research on the experiences of young people of minority or secular beliefs in Ireland (Cleary *et al.* 2001). Schools are required by law to publish their admission policy.[15] Should a school refuse to enrol a young person as a student, section 29 of the Education Act 1998 allows for an appeal by the individual or his or her parents or guardians against any such decision to the Secretary General of the Department of Education and Science. According to their deed of variation, the board of management of a denominational primary school has an obligation to uphold and foster the school's ethos (CPSMA 2000). In drawing up the school's enrolment policy, the board can use the parish

---

[14]The Department of Education and Science has increased the grant aid payable to schools that are renting temporary premises. The state is also prepared to purchase a site for a school that has demonstrated long-term viability and permanent recognition. Capital grant aid has been increased to 95 per cent of total costs and a cap has been placed on the level of local contribution (Department of Education and Science press release, 5 November 1999).

[15]Section 15, Education Act 1998.

boundary, diocesan policies or ethos considerations as enrolment criteria (CPSMA 2001). The right of schools to exercise preferential treatment regarding the admission of members of their own religious communities is recognised in the Equal Status Acts. However, the legislation cannot be interpreted as enabling schools to automatically refuse access to an individual student of a different belief to the school's particular denomination. The onus is on the school to prove that refusal of such a student is essential in order to maintain its ethos.

Perhaps one of the key equality issues for those of minority or secular beliefs attending primary or post-primary schools is the right not to participate in aspects of the life of the school that reflect a particular set of beliefs and practices. The Constitution guarantees the right of any child not to be given inappropriate religious instruction. The Introduction to the recently revised Primary Curriculum acknowledges the important contribution religious education makes to a young person's development (Department of Education and Science 1999b). It also draws attention to the need for schools to make flexible arrangements in delivering its religious education programme so that 'the beliefs and sensibilities of every child are respected' (ibid.: 58).

The problem for those with minority beliefs in majority-belief schools is that the religious dimension of a school's ethos is not necessarily confined to periods of religious instruction. Many schools use religious events to mark the start and end of the school year (Lynch and Lodge 2002). In primary or secondary schools, the religious values and practices of a given denomination are generally expected to permeate the life of the school (CPSMA 2000). In these contexts, it is far from clear how the beliefs of those from minority backgrounds are respected. While it may be easy for schools to arrange that individual students opt out of specified periods of religious instruction, it is more difficult to enable them to opt out of events that form a part of the life of the school.

In Roman Catholic primary schools, for example, preparation for religious events (First Confession, First Communion, Confirmation)[16] is an intrinsic part of the school day (Lodge 1998). Regardless of the fact that ceremonies such as the First Communion may have social and cultural meanings that may well take precedence over their religious significance

---

[16]Preparation for each of the sacraments occurs during religious instruction in Roman Catholic primary schools.

(Lodge 1999), they are religious rituals that belong to one particular set of believers. Children of minority or secular beliefs cannot fully take part in these events, yet they are often a core part of the schoolwork of particular classes over a lengthy period (ibid.). A small-scale study of the experiences of minority-belief parents of primary school children indicated that parents who are not Roman Catholic were particularly concerned about the inclusion of sacramental preparation in the school day in Roman Catholic schools. This was especially problematic for parents who had no alternative choice of school. Some parents reported that their children were isolated, teased or bullied as a result of their nonparticipation in sacramental preparation and ceremonies. Other parents anticipated these problems and selected a non-Roman Catholic school instead (Lodge 2004).

Overall it would seem that the lack of choice open to parents and young people of minority or secular beliefs or no beliefs regarding the type of school they can attend is indicative of reluctance within education in Ireland to accommodate differences in the field of religious beliefs.

The problems associated with the conflicting rights of schools to uphold their specific religious ethos and the rights of parents and students to avail of education in a manner that respects their different beliefs have only became apparent in recent times (Randles 1996; Clarke 1998). Hogan and Whyte (1994) suggest that it is only with the emergence of an increasingly secular society that challenges to state support for denominational education are becoming apparent. Whatever the historical or cultural origin, however, it would appear that the rights of individuals to religious freedom and the rights of denominational schools to uphold their ethos are currently at odds (Mullally 2001). There are questions that remain to be resolved regarding the balancing of these rights.

6.3 Diversity recognition issues

Religious education programmes in denominational primary schools are devised by the religious bodies that manage them. As almost all primary schools are denominational (with the exception of the small multidenominational sector), religious education at primary level is predominantly denominational. Religious education at second level has also been denominationally managed to date. Teacher education for religious teachers is also strongly denominational in character.

A new post-primary religious education syllabus has been introduced as part of the junior cycle programme in 350 secondary schools (Department of Education and Science 2000c). It was examined for the first time in the 2003 examination and the intention is that it will eventually be introduced in all second-level schools. A religious education programme has also been developed for the Leaving Certificate Applied (LCA) programme, and a religious education syllabus was introduced in the general Leaving Certificate in September 2003. The new post-primary religious education syllabi were designed using a consultative process involving the education partners and other interested bodies. Early drafts of the material produced were sent to representatives of the main churches as well as to religious leaders of other groups, including the Islamic and Jewish communities.[17] Various other groups, including the Baha'i community, a Buddhist organisation and the Association of Irish Humanists, were also consulted.

The religious education programmes in both the junior cycle and the Leaving Certificate Applied are Christian and monotheistic in focus. Although students have the opportunity to study other world religions, non-Christian beliefs are afforded a less significant place within the new syllabi. The syllabus for the LCA does include some reference to secular beliefs, such as the humanist perspective. However, secular beliefs are included in a section considering 'Challenges to Faith' and are examined alongside other issues such as the materialism of modern society, thereby presenting them in a negative light.

The new post-primary religion syllabi recommend that teachers should be sensitive to and aware of the diverse religious or secular beliefs in the particular group of students being taught. Given that primary teachers receive their methodological training in religious education in denominational institutions, as do most second-level teachers of religion, it is not at all clear how such teachers are prepared for this task.

The major and long-established religious denominations in Ireland have had control over religious education for their own members within schools, which has meant that what is defined as religious education has been largely education in the precepts or beliefs of a single religion. In effect, segregation of religious instruction has served to preclude conflicts over the recognition of different beliefs. Newer and less-established belief groups and groups of nonbelievers do not have the same authority or influence in either establishing schools or in framing the kind of education they want for their children in religious matters. Groups that

---

[17] Information provided by the NCCA.

are not represented by hierarchical structures similar to those of the main Christian churches or the Jewish and Islamic communities have not exercised the same influence as the established churches in education. While this is partly due to their small size, it is also related to their style of organisation. Secular groups and other belief minorities often lack the hierarchical systems of control and management that facilitate engagement with hierarchically organised school or state institutions. In addition, prevailing models of educational management have evolved from within church systems (involving a patron, local parish contributions, etc.). Groups that do not operate within such structures have no natural routes of influence within education.

6.4 Harassment

There is very little research on the experiences of those of minority or secular beliefs in Irish education, which means there is a lack of research on harassment of individuals as a result of their religious beliefs. The experiences of religious minorities and attitudes towards them formed one element of a study on the equality climates of post-primary schools (Lynch and Lodge 2002). Most of the participating students insisted that religious belief was a private matter and of no interest to them in the way that they regarded their peers. However, there were a small number of incidences reported of students who belonged to a minority denomination being teased by classmates because of their religious views (Lynch and Lodge 1999). Furthermore, where students had little or no contact with those of different beliefs, a small number expressed concern about the difficulty they would experience being friendly with or close to someone of another religion (Lodge and Lynch 2001). The latter finding would suggest that denominationally separate schooling is unhelpful in the establishment of trust between those who belong to different communities of belief. However, for some minority religious groups, separate schools may be regarded as a way of sparing their children the experiences of rejection or exclusion due to their religious or cultural identity (Milne 1996).

6.5 Good practice initiatives

- Changes in the way funding support for primary schools is structured has been a significant development in assisting groups and communities establishing schools without the institutional support of any of the main religious denominations. The Department of Education and Science has made changes to the arrangements for the purchase of a site for a school and capped the amount that the local community must contribute towards building costs (Department of Education and Science 1999c; Glendenning 1999). This initiative has been especially important to the multidenominational sector at primary level, as those wanting this education often lacked both the financial resources and institutional networks that would enable them to establish new schools, even when the demand for such schools is high. However, even where the Department of Education and Science grants recognition to a new school, it has advised the promoters since summer 2002 that a period of between seven and ten years will elapse before permanent accommodation can be provided. Over half of all multidenominational schools in operation in 2003 were awaiting permanent accommodation.

• Education provision at primary level is no longer totally denominational in nature due to the development and spread of multidenominational schools. These schools represent models of good practice by actively encouraging recognition and respect for diversity as a core principle of their ethos. The commitment of such schools to a more democratic model of management and active parental involvement is a further positive dimension.

• The development of the new religious syllabi at second level represents a move away from the traditional provision of religious instruction, replacing it with a subject that is focused on the study of religion. The syllabi formally acknowledge that there are a variety of religious beliefs and that there are people who hold secular beliefs or who do not belong to specific organised religious groups.

• The development of the new second-level religious education syllabi involved a process of consultation with the representatives of minority as well as majority religious bodies regarding curriculum development. Some consultation was also conducted with the Association of Irish Humanists on behalf of people who hold secular beliefs. The development of more inclusive practices of consultation marks a new and more pluralist approach to the development of religious education in Ireland.

Chapter 7

Age

7.1 Introduction and background information

Discrimination on the basis of age is defined in the equality legislation as treating in a comparable situation a person less favourably than another person because of a difference in their ages. The different provisions and the ages to which this protection applies are outlined in Tables 8 and 9. (It is important to note that the age limits apply to discrimination on the *age* ground and that they do not prevent a person who is outside the age limits from taking a case if they have been discriminated on any of the other grounds.)

Table 8. Some provisions in the Employment Equality Acts relating to the age ground

Age limit in the definition of discrimination on the age ground
Discrimination on the age ground under the Employment Equality Acts applies to all ages above the maximum age at which a person is statutorily obliged to attend school. (Under the Education (Welfare) Act 2000, this is set at sixteen.)

Exemptions include
An employer may require a minimum age not exceeding eighteen years in recruitment and may offer a fixed-term contract to a person who is over the compulsory retirement age.

Exemptions are provided in relation to age-based criteria for occupational benefits schemes and entitlement to benefits and severance pay, provided this does not constitute discrimination on the gender ground.

An employer can set different ages for the retirement of employees.

Anything done in compliance with the Protection of Young Persons (Employment) Act 1996, the National Minimum Wage Act 2000 or section 3 of the Redundancy Payments Act 1971 (as amended by section 5 of the Redundancy Payments Act 1979) is not discrimination on the age ground. A number of other sections of various Acts are also exempted.

An exemption applies to any term in a collective agreement, whenever made, to the effect that, in particular, where length of service would otherwise be regarded as equal, seniority in a particular post or employment may be determined by reference to the relative ages of employees on their entry to that post or employment.

Table 9. Some provisions in the Equal Status Acts relating to the age ground

---

Age limit in the definition of discrimination on the age ground
Discrimination on the age ground under the Equal Status Acts applies to all to people over eighteen (except for the provision of car insurance to licensed drivers under that age).

Exemptions include
Universities or other third-level or adult education institutions can provide different treatment in the allocation of places to mature students.

Educational establishments can provide different treatment on the age ground in relation to the provision or organisation of sporting events or facilities, but only to the extent that the differences are necessary having regard to the nature of the facilities or events.

Given that the vast majority of those engaged in compulsory education are aged under eighteen years, discrimination on the ground of age is not applicable to most school-going students. (However, there are exceptions, especially among those with an intellectual disability, many of whom may still be in school or benefit from remaining in education beyond the age of eighteen years.) This chapter therefore focuses on educational equality issues in respect of adults, with particular reference to older people where relevant. However, there is very little research in education on the issue of discrimination on the age ground per se and the analysis below is constrained by this. The issue of equality in education for older people was addressed by the Equality Authority in its report *Implementing Equality for Older People* (Equality Authority 2002b). That report makes recommendations dealing with formal education, consultation with older people and their organisations, the recognition of qualifications, education and training for work, the provision of information and the involvement of older people in the provision of education.

7.2 Presence and participation issues

Age-based differentials in educational attainment are arguably among the most persistent inequalities in industrialised countries. This also holds true for Ireland, where there are sizeable differences in the levels of general educational attainment depending on age (Table 10). For example, approximately one-third of the Irish population aged over fifty-five has

Table 10. Percentage of the population that has attained at least upper secondary and at least tertiary education, by age group and gender

Age	At least upper secondary education		At least tertiary education	
	Males	*Females*	*Males*	*Females*
25–34	71	76	45	50
35–44	59	66	37	36
45–54	46	50	30	28
55–64	35	36	22	20
25–64	**55**	**60**	**35**	**36**

Source: Education at a Glance: OECD Indicators (2002)

completed upper second-level or higher education. This is among the lowest rates for that age group in the European Union (OECD 2002).

Only six of the OECD countries have a lower rate of attainment for both genders at the at least upper secondary level in the 55–64 age group (Greece, Italy, Mexico, Portugal, Spain and Turkey), while another five have lower attainments for one gender (Austria, Canada, Iceland and Korea for females; Poland for males).

Despite (or because of) the comparative poor educational attainments of Irish adults, participation by adults in education is also comparatively low. Mature students, for example, constitute only 5 per cent of all entrants to higher education in Ireland, compared with 29 per cent in Northern Ireland and 33 per cent in Britain (Lynch 1997). The profile of mature entrants to higher education certainly indicates that it is younger 'mature students' who constitute the majority of entrants: in 1993–4, 52 per cent of all higher education mature student entrants were under thirty years of age[18], while only 5 per cent were over fifty years of age (Lynch 1997: 83–4). Furthermore, entrants from lower socio-economic groups are only marginally better represented among mature students than among school-leaver entrants (Clancy 1995; Fleming and Murphy 1997; Lynch 1997; Clancy and Wall 2000). These patterns suggest that if the educational

---

[18]One must be twenty-three years old to qualify as a mature student for higher education purposes.

needs of adults and of older people in particular are to be accommodated, new and more imaginative access routes to further and higher education need to be introduced.

People need to be highly literate and numerate to fully participate in Ireland's knowledge-based economy (Department of Education and Science 1998b). Yet reflecting these deficits in educational attainment and participation, literacy and numeracy levels among Irish adults give cause for concern, especially among older age groups and among those who are poor (Bailey and Coleman 1998). The International Literacy Survey found that one-quarter of Irish adults have difficulties with the simplest literacy tasks (Morgan *et al.* 1997), with Irish adults performing particularly poorly in comparison with those in other industrialised nations – only Poland had lower scores. Only one-sixth of Irish adults surveyed were at the highest literacy levels, compared with one-third of those in Sweden.

There is a range of educational options open to adults, including third level, vocational training, further and continuing education and a variety of adult and community education courses. However, while most adults are not excluded from returning to education on age grounds, many are indirectly precluded from accessing education because of other barriers.

A general problem identified is the difficulty that adults encounter in accessing accurate information about the possible courses, options and types of assistance open to them (Fleming and Murphy 1997; Healy 1998; Inglis and Murphy 1999; NALA 2001). Many adults who may wish to return to education cannot access the relevant information, as there is no national network for disseminating information about different types of adult, community, continuing or further education. While there are specific kinds of information available (such as the Department of Education and Science's booklet on the full-time undergraduate courses open to adults in third-level college), this type of information is quite specialised and is generally only available in print form. There is also no national guidance service for adult returnees to enable them to choose appropriate courses.

While the lack of information is a major problem for those who are Irish or who have spent a significant amount of time in Ireland, it is an even bigger problem for the new minority ethnic groups. What information is available is generally only available in English and there is no particular structure for making information available to minority linguistic or ethnic groups. Moreover, apart from the provision of English classes, the adult and further education needs of the new communities have not been addressed.

A second constraint for adults returning to education is the lack of flexibility in access routes. Third-level education offers the most valuable rewards at degree and diploma levels. It is also generously resourced in terms of state investment compared with other educational sectors (OECD 1998; Archer 2001). Yet access to third level remains relatively difficult for all mature entrants, with competitive entry based on the Leaving Certificate being the standard route of entry (Higher Education Authority 1995; Hannan *et al.* 1998). The Leaving Certificate examination is widely used as a selection mechanism for apprenticeships and Post-Leaving Certificate courses (Smyth and Hannan 2000; Archer 2001). Yet there is a sizeable proportion of older people (39 per cent of the 50–59 year olds, for example) who have not even completed second-level education (OECD 2000). Systems of acquired prior learning (APL) and acquired prior experiential learning (APEL) should be developed to allow older learners to access education opportunities, especially within higher education. This would enable those who have previously benefited least from the education system to gain access to training and qualifications. The National Qualifications Authority of Ireland (2003) has begun work on addressing this issue.

Socio-economic factors in particular continue to play an important role in influencing access to and participation in education. Among all age groups, it is people from working-class and lower socio-economic backgrounds who are the least likely to stay in school to complete the Leaving Certificate, and even when they do they are the least likely to perform well (OECD 1995; Hannan *et al.* 1996; McCoy *et al.* 1999; Smyth 1999). Given the lack of alternative second-chance access routes to education, it is not surprising that those who already have qualifications are the most likely to engage in further certified education or training (Hannan and Doyle 2000). Adults from working-class and other lower socio-economic groups are still substantially less likely to attend third-level institutions, particularly universities, than are their peers from middle- and upper middle-class backgrounds (Morris 1997).

Women are underrepresented among mature students in higher education, especially among part-time students (Lynch 1997; McMinn 2000). A number of direct and indirect barriers have been identified for adult women returning to education. Among these is their dependent status in the tax and social welfare codes, with the attendant consequence that they lack independent financial means to access education when and if they wish to avail of it. Women also take a disproportionately high level of responsibility for all types of care work in our society. The lack of adequate child care supports is a major barrier to education for women with dependent children, as is the general lack of care support services.

Financial constraints are also a significant problem for many potential students of further and continuing education. *Learning for Life: White Paper on Adult Education* has acknowledged the impact of financial constraints (Department of Education and Science 2000a). It noted that most of the submissions received had made a case for the provision of free access to different forms of adult education.

There are a number of schemes available to assist mature students who are socially excluded in accessing third-level education. The Back to Education Allowance (BTEA) scheme is designed to support those wishing to attend second or third level who are unemployed, lone parents or persons with disabilities (VTOS 2002). Yet there is a range of different restrictions on qualifying for the Back to Education Allowance, including the fact that the age limits differ depending on circumstances, such as whether the applicant has a disability or is in receipt of different welfare allowances.

Overall, these barriers are less important outside the formal education sectors. There is a wide variety of educational options in the community and adult education sector, although it is difficult to get accurate data on the nature and scope of these initiatives. They are highly diverse in character and organised by a wide range of different organisations. However, while many forms of second-chance, adult and community education are more financially accessible, they often provide limited options for progression to further education, with many courses remaining unaccredited. These problems are exacerbated by the lack of a standard national system for accrediting prior learning. However, these issues have begun to be addressed since the establishment of the National Council for Vocational Awards and the development by the National Qualifications Authority of a National Framework of Qualifications and a related framework for access, transfer and progression.

A study on the educational needs of those aged fifty-five and over found that there was broad agreement between people in that age group and educational service providers that their needs were very poorly catered for (Boldt 1998). Specific provision aimed at older people is generally provided by voluntary bodies associated to the Federation of Active Retirement Associations; however, given the voluntary nature of these organisations, the range of possible courses is limited and they are not accredited (Boldt 1998; Ryan 1998). Therefore, while these courses undoubtedly address a social need, they do not provide older people with the opportunity to acquire further educational qualifications.

Nevertheless, adult and community education constitutes a vital part of the educational infrastructure for adults, especially for those who are socially or economically marginalised. However, it is generally poorly resourced, particularly in the community sector (McMinn 2000). Much time and energy in community groups is spent submitting proposals for funding rather than planning and running education programmes. As it is the more educationally marginalised groups in society that avail of community education in particular, the failure to support it compounds prior injustices.

7.3 Good practice initiatives

• The setting up of the National Council for Vocational Awards to develop an accreditation system for courses and programmes outside the more traditional structures of education is a welcome initiative. It will develop systems of accreditation for courses and for prior learning that have not been accredited to date. It will also be able to provide a framework for progression between courses and programmes.

• Mature students themselves have identified access and induction courses as one of the most positive developments in higher education (Fleming and Murphy 1997). Such programmes have been found to be especially valuable for those from socio-economically disadvantaged backgrounds. While most third-level institutions provide support for mature students, not all colleges have a full-time permanent member of staff specifically employed to mentor and take responsibility for the needs of this group.

• The Vocational Training Opportunities Scheme (VTOS) has specifically targeted excluded groups, including lone parents, people with disabilities and those who are unemployed, to assist their access to second- and third-level education as mature students.

- The adult and community sector offers examples of innovative and adult learner-oriented educational models. Furthermore, it offers support and affirmation to socially excluded groups, such as women experiencing poverty and isolation (McMinn 2000). *Learning for Life: White Paper on Adult Education* praised the community education sector, particularly women's community education, for its participant-directed, emancipatory dimension and promised to increase funding to this area (Department of Education and Science 2000a). However, community education remains a substantially underresourced area. It has not been assessed or researched to the degree that it deserves.

- The National Women's Council of Ireland initiated a national research, analysis and action study to mark the millennium. One dimension of this project focused on women's educational needs and experiences. This research was learning focused and set out to connect the experiences of women taking part in community education and those who make local, regional and national policy. All participants were learners in the process (National Women's Council of Ireland 2001). This type of research project provides a model for engaging adult learners in research in a way that is respectful and potentially emancipatory.

- *Learning for Life: White Paper on Adult Education* set out structures to be established at both local and national level (Department of Education and Science 2000a). Given that much of further and continuing education in Ireland has been organised on an *ad hoc* basis to date, the proposed establishment of structures such as the National Adult Learning Council and Local Adult Learning Boards is to be welcomed. It is proposed that Local Adult Learning Boards will include representatives from the social partners and learners alongside education providers. However, as O'Riordan (2001) points out, it is disappointing that there has been no move towards activating these structures to date.

- The review of the senior cycle of post-primary education includes a proposal to develop a Leaving Certificate Applied course for the adult and continuing education sector.[19] While this is to be welcomed, it must be borne in mind that third-level institutions do not currently recognise the Leaving Certificate Applied for competitive entry purposes.

[19]Information supplied by NCCA.

Chapter 8
Race

8.1 Introduction and background information

The equality legislation defines the race ground in terms of race, skin colour, nationality or national or ethnic origin. The definition of the race ground has a number of elements that can give rise to different issues. Nationality is specifically referred to in some of the formal legal rights and administrative policies concerning access to or participation in education, but race, skin colour or ethnic origin are not. On the other hand, race, skin colour and ethnic origin can arise in the context of recognising and accommodating diversity and this has implications for equality in the education system. Some of the particular exemptions that apply to the race ground to be found in the Employment Equality Acts and the Equal Status Acts, respectively, are given in Tables 11 and 12. A Traveller ground is defined separately from the race ground. Travellers are also covered by the race ground, but for this report Traveller issues are dealt with in a separate chapter.

Table 11. A provision in the Employment Equality Acts relating to the race ground

---

Exemptions include
Any action taken in accordance with the Employment Permits Act 2003.

In recent years education policy has begun to acknowledge and develop a range of antiracist, intercultural and equality commitments. *The National Children's Strategy: Our Children – Their Lives* (Department of Health and Children 2000: 70) contains the key objective that 'children will be educated and supported to value social and cultural diversity so that all children including Travellers and other marginalised groups achieve their

Table 12. Some provisions in the Equal Status Acts relating to the race ground

Exemptions include

Institutions providing adult, continuing or further education or universities or other third-level institutions can treat nationals of an EU member state differently from those who are not in relation to fees for admission or attendance and the allocation of places.

The Minister for Education and Science can require grants to be restricted to nationals of an EU member state or can require such nationals to be treated differently in relation to making grants.

Different treatment is allowed by vocational and training bodies in relation to fees and the allocation of places to people who are nationals of an EU member state.

Public authorities can treat certain non-nationals differently on the basis of their nationality. This applies (a) to those who are outside the state or who are (for the purposes of the Immigration Act 2004) unlawfully present in it or (b) in accordance with any provision or condition made by or under any enactment and arising from the non-national's entry to or residence in the state.

Universities and other third-level college or adult educational institutions can allocate places for exchange students.

full potential.' *Charting Our Education Future: White Paper on Education* noted that 'the democratic character of this society requires education to embrace the diverse traditions, beliefs and values of its people' (Department of Education 1995: 5). It identified 'the importance of education in areas such as human rights, tolerance, mutual understanding [and] cultural identity.' The Department of Education and Science's submission to the preparation of the National Action Plan on Racism, *Promoting Anti-Racism and Interculturalism in Education* (Department of Education and Science 2002b), noted the need for an educational response to the suspicion that exists in Irish society towards ethnic diversity. The purpose of this response is 'to promote acceptance of this rapid social change, a climate of respect for the rights of all, and a welcome for ethnic diversity.' Other major education policy statements that discuss the need for education policy and practice to address racism and interculturalism include *Ready to Learn: White Paper on Early Childhood* (Department of Education and Science 1999f) and *Learning for Life: White Paper on Adult Education* (Department of Education and Science 2000a).

The linguistic and cultural origins of minority ethnic groups in Ireland to date – predominantly white English speakers from the UK, US, etc. – has meant that there has been very little research into the educational experiences of these groups other than studies on Travellers and education (Kenny 1997). The changing profile of immigrants in the second half of the 1990s has resulted in a growing interest in multiculturalism and educational provision for minority ethnic groups. Much of this recent work has focused on asylum seekers and refugees (McGovern 1990; INTO 1998; Broderick 2000; Fanning *et al.* 2000, 2001; Faughnan and Woods 2000; Murray 2000).

However, there are other minority ethnic groups availing of education in Ireland. Freedom of movement between European Union member states has resulted in an increasing number of European Union citizens coming to live, work and study in Ireland. Economic growth has also meant that there is an increase in the number of foreign nationals being issued with work visas and permits. Irish third-level colleges and language institutes actively seek international students, which is also changing the ethnic profile of the resident population, and the limited research available suggests that such students also experience racism and discrimination (Boucher 1998).

As the equality concerns of minority ethnic groups in education have not been researched in depth in Ireland, the discussion below is curtailed by the limited nature of the available research material. The experiences of members of the Traveller community are dealt with in Chapter 10.

8.2 Presence and participation issues

To date, specific data on ethnicity, other than membership of the Traveller community, has not been collected in the census or national sample surveys. Data on nationality collected in the 2002 census shows that of a total population of 3,858,495, some 224,261 people (5.8 per cent of the total population) were of non-Irish nationality. Of these, 133,346 (3.5 per cent) were from the fourteen other EU countries. There is limited official data on ethnic or national minorities in Irish education because very little disaggregation of data on ethnic grounds occurs (RAXEN 3).[20] While the age groupings used in the published census figures do not match the age

---

[20]The source is a RAXEN 3 study entitled *Analytical Study on Education* for the European Monitoring Centre on Racism and Xenophobia (EUMC), Vienna, Austria (forthcoming).

of compulsory education, published data on those aged zero to fourteen years (given in Table 13) shows that there were 34,131 children of nationalities other than Irish in the population. In addition, of those whose primary nationality was given as Irish, 15,755 children reported a second nationality.

The rest of this section looks first at the situation of children and then that of adults.

Table 13. Persons aged 0–14 usually resident and present in the state on census night 2002, classified by nationality

Irish	759,848
Irish-English	5,314
Irish-American	3,731
Irish-European	2,429
Irish-Other	4,281
Total Irish	**775,603**
UK	17,220
Other EU	2,038
Non-EU European	2,773
Africa	4,305
Asia	1,888
America	4,348
Australia and New Zealand	764
Other nationalities	323
Multi nationality	472
Total Non-Irish	**34,131**
No nationality stated	229
Not stated	13,916
Total	**823,879**

Source: Census 2002 – Principal Demographic Results

Children

Under the Education (Welfare) Act 2000, children in Ireland between the ages of six and sixteen are subject to compulsory education. (This Act came into force in July 2002. Among other provisions, it replaced previous legislation that had set an upper age of fourteen for compulsory education.) The provision on compulsory education applies regardless of the legal status of the young person, that is, it applies to Irish nationals and foreign nationals; to those who are living in the country on the basis of a legal right (for example, under EU law); to those whose families are here on the basis of a visa or work permit; to those who are refugees; and to those who have applied for asylum but whose application has not yet been decided upon.

Language difficulties due to lack of familiarity with English represent particular barriers to full participation in education for some minority ethnic groups. In March 1999 the Department of Education and Science set up the Refugee Language Support Unit as a two-year pilot project under the Centre for Language and Communication Studies at Trinity College, Dublin. In July 1999 Interact Ireland (formerly the Refugee Language and Training Project) merged with the Refugee Language Support Unit. This was a two-year EU-funded partnership project, the purpose of which was to promote the integration of refugees in Irish society through linked language and vocational training (Integrate Ireland Language and Training 2002). At the end of this pilot project, English language proficiency benchmarks were developed for the adult sector (vocational and prevocational) and for the school sector (primary and post-primary). (A second outcome was the design and delivery of English language courses appropriate to the needs of adult refugees.) Materials and in-service training to support primary and post-primary teachers were also developed. In September 2001 the Refugee Language Support Unit became Integrate Ireland Language and Training Ltd, a not-for-profit campus company of Trinity College, Dublin. Integrate Ireland Language and Training Ltd has been allocated funding by the Department of Education and Science for the duration of the National Development Plan 2000–2006 (Integrate Ireland Language and Training 2002).

Differences in the levels of support offered to children depending on their status as refugees or as asylum seekers was highlighted by the Irish National Teachers' Organization (INTO 1998: 38–40). At that time, policy on language supports in education had been developed in the specific context of promoting integration for those who are recognised as refugees. In 2000 the Department of Education and Science published an undated guide for schools that indicated that language supports do not distinguish between the different legal statuses of the school students (Department of Education and Science, no date).

In the primary sector, schools with an enrolment of fourteen or more foreign nationals with English language deficits are entitled to an additional teacher, appointed on a year-by-year basis, to provide language support for such pupils. An individual child is entitled to a maximum of two years of language support. These appointments are temporary. In the case of a school having twenty-eight or more non-English-speaking foreign nationals, the school is entitled to a second additional teacher. Where a full-time teacher is sanctioned to provide English language support, a start-up grant of €635 is paid; €317 is paid where the appointment is continued for a further year. In the 2001–02 school year, approximately 144 posts were sanctioned (Department of Education and Science 2003a: 9). In the 2003–04 school year, the number of teacher posts sanctioned was 479.[21]

In primary schools where the number of eligible pupils is less than fourteen, grants are paid to enable the school authorities to arrange for part-time teaching for these pupils. The grants are at two levels and are available to any school that has three or more such pupils enrolled to enable them to acquire the services of a suitable person to teach these pupils English (Department of Education and Science 2003a: 9–10). A primary school catering for one or two such children must provide for these pupils' language needs out of existing resources unless this presents a particular difficulty.

In some schools individual teachers have given English language support and teaching to foreign national children on a voluntary basis (Broderick 2000). However, there is evidence that in other schools, language difficulties are used as a reason to refuse to enrol children or are the cause of a child experiencing exclusion and segregation in classrooms.

The impact of the home environment and disadvantaged living conditions on children's participation and progress in school is widely recognised. This issue is also of relevance for those asylum seekers who are recent arrivals and are subject to direct provision, that is, they are required to live in designated accommodation, which can be crowded and inappropriate for families. Furthermore, they have very little money available for expenses of any kind, including educational needs (Fanning *et al.* 2001). While it is true that children and young people who are foreign nationals are entitled to apply for free books and other grants on the same basis as Irish nationals (Broderick 2000), there are other hidden

---

[21]Information supplied by A. Scott, Inspectorate of the Department of Education and Science, February 2004.

costs associated with school that are not provided for in the allowance system, including all types of extracurricular activities, cultural events, etc. As Fanning *et al.* (2001) point out, hostel accommodation does not allow for privacy; thus it presents difficulties in terms of a quiet place to study. Lack of access to transport or difficulties due to costs have an impact on parental choices regarding appropriate schools and preschools for their children. Broderick (2000), whose study looked at the asylum system in Ireland, argues that children of asylum seekers can experience indirect discrimination in accessing primary or post-primary education due to lack of parental knowledge of systems of enrolment and due to stipulations regarding catchment areas or links with designated feeder schools. Two Separated Children Education Officers with the City of Dublin VEC and County Dublin VEC work with unaccompanied minors and schools to ensure appropriate placements.

Two further particular issues arise for many children from minority ethnic groups in Irish schools: recognition of their social and cultural differences, which is dealt with below in section 8.3, and religious differences. A large number of schools in Ireland are denominational and the Education Act 1998 gives them the right to protect their religious ethos. This can be a barrier to full equality for those members of minority ethnic groups whose religious beliefs are not catered for by the Irish education system or whose circumstances make it impossible for them to access a school that does cater for their religious belief. (These issues are discussed in more detail in Chapter 6 on religion.)

Adults

Most categories of adults, e.g. overseas students in third-level colleges, members of long-established minority ethnic groups, citizens of other EU countries, do not face direct barriers in terms of accessing education and training, nor do they necessarily experience financial barriers to their full participation in education. Overall, while there is a lack of clarity regarding the educational rights and entitlements of foreign nationals, there appears to be no formal prohibition to the participation of most non-Irish adults in the state in education and training, although asylum seekers may have restrictions on their participation in education before their application for refugee status is decided upon. Asylum seekers who complete the Leaving Certificate (along with other inward migrants who have spent less then three years in the state) are not allowed to take up third-level places (Irish Refugee Council 2004). One specific exemption in the Equal Status Acts permits differences in treatment in adult, continuing or further education and in third-level institutions between those who are EU nationals or refugees and those who are not. The differences allowed cover fees and the allocation of places.

Those who are present in the state on the basis of a work visa or work authorisation may participate in education, but they have not been entitled to state support such as maintenance grants. In May 2003 the Equality Tribunal found a rule that restricts eligibility for maintenance grants for Post-Leaving Certificate courses to EU nationals, refugees and those granted humanitarian leave to remain to be discriminatory. A provision of the Equality Act 2004 overturned the applicability of this decision to future cases.

A particular issue that has been identified in the context of adult learners is access to language support. Even if non-Irish adults have the right to participate in education and training, they may lack the language skills to enable them to do so. However, those adults who are recognised refugees or who have been given leave to remain are entitled to English language training through the VECs and Integrate Ireland Language and Training Ltd.

Until late 2001 asylum-seeker adults were not entitled to state-funded language classes and had been reliant on those classes provided by voluntary bodies (Fanning *et al.* 2001). The classes that asylum seekers attended were run by voluntary organisations such as the Irish Refugee Council and various religious organisations (Cullen 2000; Faughnan and Woods 2000). Reports of the standards of such voluntary language classes indicate that not all were meeting the needs of asylum seekers (Faughan and Woods 2000; Fanning *et al.* 2001). *Learning for Life: White Paper on Adult Education* contains a plan to extend state-funded English language classes to asylum seekers as well as enabling those with the right to work to take part in vocational training programmes (Department of Education and Science 2000a). In late 2001 the Department of Education and Science advised VECs that funds allocated to them by the Department for their adult literacy services could also be used to provide English language classes to adult asylum seekers who require such classes. Up to the end of 2003, 5,928 clients availed of English as a second language (ESL) courses provided by the VECs. However, it is worth noting that although asylum seekers can access these courses without charge, they will not be able to get a grant to enable them to take part in full-time courses.

As a number of different studies have demonstrated, foreign nationals have difficulty in getting their existing qualifications recognised (Sherlock 2002). This limits their ability to participate in further education and training, including the upgrading of their qualifications in order to improve their chances of gaining appropriate employment (Fanning *et al.* 2000).

8.3 Diversity recognition issues

The National Co-ordinating Committee of the 1997 European Year Against Racism (1998) noted that schools have a vital role to play in addressing racism and lack of respect for ethnic difference with all students. Lack of curricular recognition for ethnic difference can operate as a further barrier to full participation for learners. There are a number of subjects specifically concerned with issues of social justice and respect for differences, including ethnic difference. The Social, Political and Health Education (SPHE) curriculum (taught in primary schools and in the junior cycle at post-primary) fosters respect for oneself and others, as well as promoting awareness for and recognition of cultural difference.

Civic, Social and Political Education (CSPE) is underpinned by a concern for issues of social justice and human rights. In theory there is scope to introduce issues of concern to minority ethnic groups, but in practice this is more difficult. CSPE is provided only to junior cycle post-primary students; there is no comparable programme for primary pupils. The provision of CSPE actually declines for many students between first and third year (Department of Education and Science 1999d), thus the subject is afforded little opportunity to address a wide range of issues in any depth. Furthermore, as there is no CSPE programme at senior cycle, the themes around citizenship cannot be developed and built upon at more sophisticated levels. In addition, to date there is little focus on the rights or experiences of minority ethnic groups in the exemplar material provided for teachers of either the SPHE or CSPE programmes.

The fact that subjects such as SPHE and CSPE exist and have a specific focus on, respect for and recognition of difference, including ethnic difference, is to be welcomed. Other subjects, such as the history component of the revised primary curriculum, also offer the possibility of focusing on different cultures and their histories as well as on the story of Ireland. However, as the teacher guidelines note:

> This flexibility places an onus on teachers to plan a history
> programme that reflects the needs and organisation of their school

71

and ensure that children will study elements from early, middle and modern periods and from local, national and international contexts (Department of Education and Science 1999b: 19).

As Witcher (1984) has observed, teachers' attitudes are central to the successful communication of an antisexist curriculum. The same arguments can be applied to the successful teaching of a curriculum that is inclusive and respects ethnic difference.

The National Council for Curriculum and Assessment (NCCA) has appointed two education officers with responsibility for intercultural education and is devising guidelines to help teachers to adapt the existing curriculum to meet the needs of an ethnically diverse student population.[22] *Learning for Life: White Paper on Adult Education* noted that curriculum training, in-service training and assessment should be devised and put into operation within an intercultural rather than a monocultural framework (Department of Education and Science 2000a). This is equally applicable to all levels of education.

8.4 Harassment

There is abundant evidence from other ethnically diverse education systems of bullying and harassment of those students belonging to minority ethnic groups (Mac an Ghaill 1994; Mason 1995). There is little available research on the extent of racist behaviour and harassment in Irish educational institutions, but the emerging research evidence is not encouraging. Both the study by Fanning *et al.* (2001) of children in schools and the study by Boucher (1998) of students in universities found evidence of individual and institutional prejudice and discrimination on the grounds of ethnicity and skin colour. In addition, the attitudes of young people in second-level schools towards refugees and asylum seekers have not been found to be positive or pluralist (Keogh 2000). A study of the experiences of 'mixed race' Irish people describes exclusion and lack of respect for difference across a range of institutions, including schools (McCarthy 2001). The documented experience of Travellers in education and other institutions also shows a marked failure to respect their cultural differences (Kenny 1997). Even individual students with distinct accents or lifestyles can experience verbal abuse

---

[22]Information provided by the NCCA.

and bullying by their peers due to their difference (Lynch and Lodge 1999; Lodge and Lynch 2001). A recent study of attitudes towards international students in a second-level school found evidence of abusive behaviour by students from the majority group that included racist comments and threatening messages sent anonymously by mobile phone (Malone 2002). Teachers in another recent study expressed uncertainty as to how they should handle overt individual racism, such as comments made in class (Devine *et al.* 2004). Finally, there is evidence that teachers in primary and post-primary schools may inadvertently exclude some students from minority ethnic groups due to perceived English language difficulties or a lack of training or support in how best to help these young people (Fanning *et al.* 2001).

The lack of attention to the position of minority ethnic groups in higher education in Ireland led to the organisation of a conference on this topic by the Higher Education Equality Unit in 1996. Following this conference, an Advisory Group was established in order to make recommendations regarding staff and students in colleges who belonged to minority ethnic groups (Egan 1997). The conference report noted that Irish-born students from minority ethnic groups in colleges experienced racism, discrimination and harassment similar to that experienced by those from overseas. It is ironic that while colleges actively seek overseas students because they are a source of revenue, such students can be subjected to harassment and lack of institutional support. The Higher Education Authority has also noted that racism and lack of intercultural awareness are threats to the expansion of the overseas education sector at third level and has recommended that any third-level institution wishing to engage in the promotion of Irish higher education to overseas students should develop strategic plans that would cover, among other issues, pastoral and student services and wider intercultural issues (Higher Education Authority 2003: 167).

8.5 Employment equality issues

The main documented employment equality issue for people from minority ethnic groups is the difficulty they experience in gaining recognition for their qualifications (Fanning *et al.* 2000; Faughnan and Woods 2000; Sherlock 2002). To be employed as a teacher in a primary or post-primary school, an individual must apply to the Teaching Registration Council, giving details of their qualifications. If these are regarded as appropriate, an individual seeking employment in the post-primary sector does not have to meet Irish language requirements, as was the case previously. At primary level, the Irish language requirements remain – those individuals whose qualifications are recognised for primary teaching are given provisional recognition and must gain proficiency in Irish within three years. Employment in third-level institutions is also contingent on the recognition of qualifications.

There are relatively few difficulties in the recognition of qualifications between EU member states or with North American qualifications. However, for many foreign nationals, particularly those who come to Ireland as refugees or asylum seekers, gaining recognition of their qualifications is a difficult process (Faughnan and Woods 2000). Furthermore, some foreign nationals are also faced with English language difficulties.

Given the denominational nature of much of the compulsory education sector, particularly at primary level, individuals belonging to minority ethnic groups who express minority beliefs may experience difficulties in gaining employment.

8.6 Good practice initiatives

- The resource pack produced for Antiracism in the Workplace Week, *Supporting an Anti-Racist Workplace* (Equality Authority, IBEC, ICTU and CIF 2000), provides a good example of how to frame proactive, antiracist working environments, much of which can be adapted or used for information by schools. Among its suggestions is a set of core guiding principles to help create an antiracist working environment and a list of suggested workplace activities and development strategies.

- Individual schools have devised their own antiracist strategies and programmes (Murray 2000) aimed at raising the awareness of all members of the school community regarding issues of racism and respect for diversity.

- The inclusion of subjects such as SPHE in both primary and post-primary curricula and the development of CSPE, both of which include a focus on social justice and foster the recognition of and respect for difference, represents a positive opportunity to include issues such as racism and the rights of minority groups generally within compulsory education.

- In other countries there have been programmes and targets set for the creation of racism-free schools. Similar initiatives and strategies can be planned and implemented in the Irish context.

- Sets of guidelines to help teachers create classrooms that celebrate and value ethnic differences have been produced by the Irish National Teachers' Organization (INTO 2002), by LYNS (a joint committee of the Joint Managerial Body and the Association of Community and Comprehensive Schools) and jointly by the Targeting Educational Disadvantage Programme (TED) and the Centre for Educational Disadvantage Research (CEDR) in Mary Immaculate College, Limerick. The INTO document, published in 2002, is entitled *INTO Intercultural Guidelines for Schools: Valuing Difference, Combating Racism, Promoting Inclusiveness and Equality.* The LYNS report is entitled *Intercultural Education Guidelines for Schools* and was published in 2003. The TED–CEDR document, published in 2003, is entitled *Celebrating Difference, Promoting Equality: Intercultural Education in the Primary Classroom.*

- The Curriculum Development Unit of the City of Dublin VEC led work on developing a set of modules in intercultural studies, which were launched by the Further Education Training Awards Council in 2003.

- The inclusion of interculturalism as a core principle in *Learning for Life: White Paper on Adult Education* (Department of Education and Science 2000a) is to be welcomed. The White Paper requires that all publicly supported or funded adult education programmes will have to demonstrate their openness and contribution to Ireland's development as an intercultural society.

- The Irish Vocational Education Association has published two reports that address the educational needs of asylum seekers, refugees and minority linguistic groups: *IVEA Policy on Educational Provision for Asylum Seekers, Refugees and Other Non-nationals* and *Pilot Framework for Educational Provision for Asylum Seekers, Refugees and Minority Linguistic Groups.*

- The Skilbeck (2002) report on Irish universities suggests that colleges need to encourage diversity in their student and staff population. This is a welcome proposal, as it underscores the importance of having students and staff from diverse cultural and social backgrounds in higher education.

- Universities and other Higher Education Authority-designated institutions are engaged in initiatives that include antiracism, awareness raising and training and the extension of existing initiatives to support learners to include members of the Traveller community and other minority ethnic groups.

- The European Council on Refugees and Exiles (ECRE) has identified models of good practice for making education systems more accessible to refugees and asylum seekers. The provision of language teaching and support, with a guaranteed minimum number of free tuition hours, is recommended as part of the integration process. The commitment given to the support of language services (ELT) for adults and young people in the refugee communities in the National Development Plan 2000–2006 (Government of Ireland 2000) is in line with the ECRE recommendations. It should be noted, however, that this budget is a very small one.

Chapter 9
Disability

9.1 Introduction and background information

Disability is defined in the Equal Status Acts to mean the total or partial absence of a person's bodily or mental functions; the presence of organisms causing or likely to cause chronic disease or illness; the malfunction, malformation or disfigurement of a part of a person's body; a condition or malfunction which results in a person learning differently; or a condition, disease or illness which affects a person's thought process, perception of reality, emotions or judgement or which results in disturbed behaviour. A similar definition is given in the Employment Equality Acts. Discrimination on the disability ground occurs when one person is treated in a comparable situation less favourably than another person on the basis that one has a disability and the other does not or has a different disability. Important provisions in the equality legislation concern *reasonable accommodation* for people with disabilities, the details of which are given in Table 14.

Table 14. **Provisions concerning reasonable accommodation for people with disabilities in the equality legislation**

Employment Equality Acts
An employer is obliged to take appropriate measures to enable a person who has a disability to have access to employment, to participate or advance in employment or to undertake training unless the measures would impose a disproportionate burden on the employer.

Equal Status Acts
Service providers, including educational establishments, must do all that is reasonable to accommodate the needs of a person with a disability. This involves providing special treatment or facilities in circumstances where without these it would be impossible or unduly difficult to avail of the matters provided by the service provider or educational establishment. However, service providers are not obliged to provide special treatment or facilities that cost more than nominal cost.

The provisions of the Equal Status Acts rest on a presumption of mainstreaming for students with disabilities. A school is exempt from the requirement to provide service to a student with a disability only to the extent that doing so would (because of the student's disability) either (a) have a seriously detrimental effect of the provision of service to other students or (b) would make it impossible to provide services to other students.

A medical model of disability is primarily used in equality legislation and is also used in the Education Act 1998. The definition that has been used is a genuine attempt to ensure that specific disabilities are addressed. In its report *A Strategy for Equality: Report of the Commission on the Status of People with Disabilities*, the Commission on the Status of People with Disabilities (1996) recommended that legislation and policy be informed by a social model of disability within a civil rights perspective based on principles of equality and human rights. The core benefit of a social model of disability is that it would capture the complex intersection of physical, psychological and social factors in the life experience of disabled people. It would also engage with the disabling implications of law and policy that turn impairments into deprivations and barriers to equal citizenship.

The historical experience of exclusion (which had often been supported by legislation) has been vigorously challenged in recent times through campaigns by people with disabilities for rights to 'common and equal citizenship' (Quinn 1993). Insistence on use of the terms 'people with disabilities' or 'disabled people' is a strategy to promote inclusive policy and practice on a human rights basis. It indicates that service users are agents rather than objects. It has gradually been recognised that disability is often experienced in terms of the 'disabling environment', acknowledging the impact of physical and attitudinal barriers on the disabled person's ability to fully participate in society (Finkelstein and Stuart 1996).

The Education Act 1998 repeatedly states that education users include those with a disability. The Minister is required to ensure that each person is provided with an appropriate quality and level of education to meet their needs and abilities. The Act defines 'support services' for disabled students as including assessment, psychological services, guidance and counselling services, adaptations to the built environment, transport, provision for formal education outside schools and supports for specific pedagogic processes. However, there are also limits placed on the extent to which institutions are actually obliged to provide for these needs.

Frequent references to the availability of resources as a determining factor in providing adequate services and facilities for disabled learners can be found throughout the Education Act.

As Mullally (2001) points out, the rights of private property as guaranteed in the Constitution have been given precedence over the rights of those with disabilities. There is a strong arguable case that without constitutional change the rights of private property will continue to be prioritised over other rights, including the rights of those with disabilities (Lynch and Connelly 1996). However, there is no legal impediment to the state introducing civil rights-based legislation guaranteeing the rights of those with disabilities to free and appropriate education.[23, 24]

9.2 Presence and participation issues

Traditionally, many Irish people with disabilities were segregated in schools, care institutions and hospitals for much of their lives (McDonnell 2002). Within education, all children were categorised as either 'handicapped' or 'normal'. Separate educational provision was made for each group until the late 1970s and 1980s, a practice that operated not only in Ireland, but also internationally (Glendenning 1999; Egan 2000). For example, a report on the education of those with hearing impairments prepared in the early 1970s recommended that education for young people with hearing impairments should mainly occur in specialist, segregated schools (Department of Education 1972). The practice of segregation was regarded by service providers and professionals as the most appropriate way of meeting their needs (Glendenning 1999; Kenny *et al.* 2000). As recently as 1995, *Charting Our Education Future: White Paper on Education* (Department of Education 1995) prescribed a modified form of segregation. It proposed that certain schools would be 'designated' as having special responsibility for students with disabilities. By default, this meant that most schools were

---

[23]Information provided by Professor Gerard Quinn, Law Department, NUI Galway.

[24]After this chapter was written and before this report went to press, the Education for Persons with Special Educational Needs Act 2004 was passed. It establishes the principle of inclusive education for children with special educational needs as a legal requirement. The Act sets out procedures for conducting assessments of students who have special educational needs and preparing education plans for them. It also permits the designation of the school at which a child with special educational needs is to be educated. Although the Act itself is now law, it will be implemented on a phased basis over a period of at most five years. The National Council for Special Educational Needs, which is established under the Act, is required to prepare a report setting out what needs to be done for the Act to be fully implemented.

not required to be inclusive. From the perspective of many disabled people, however, segregation exaggerated their isolation and reinforced their relative invisibility (McDonnell 2002).

Increased attention was given to disability issues in education in the 1990s. The first major government-sponsored report was published in 1993, the *Special Education Review Committee Report*. The report of the Commission on the Status of People with Disabilities, *A Strategy for Equality* (1996), and the National Council for Curriculum and Assessment's discussion document, *Special Educational Needs: Curriculum Issues* (1999), were also published. Integrated provision has also been promoted (Butler and Shevlin 2001). Now education for those with disabilities includes integrated placement of disabled students in mainstream classes, as well as the more traditional provision in special schools and special classes. Of course, true integration requires much more than simply placing students with special needs in mainstream classrooms, although the changing pattern on placement does give an indication of trends.

Under the Equal Status Acts a school must provide reasonable accommodation – special treatment, facilities or adjustments – to meet the needs of a person with a disability if it would be impossible or unduly difficult for that person to participate in school without such special treatment, facilities or adjustments. There is no obligation to provide special treatment, facilities or adjustments if they give rise to anything more than a 'nominal cost'. The meaning of 'nominal cost' will depend on the circumstances of the individual service provider concerned – a large and well-resourced organisation is more likely to be able to afford a higher level of cost in making reasonable accommodation than a small one is. As most schools are funded by the state, this would suggest the 'nominal cost' exemption may not be very significant in practice. The availability of grants is an element that has to be taken into account in addressing the requirement to reasonably accommodate pupils with disabilities.

Primary education

An increasing number of primary school children with disabilities are opting to attend mainstream rather than segregated schooling. As Table 15 suggests, the proportion of children with disabilities attending special schools has dropped since 1994, and there is a noticeable rise in the number of young people with disabilities enrolled in mainstream primary

Table 15. Percentage of pupils categorised as disabled in primary schools, by school type during 1994–5, 1998–9 and 2001–02

School year	In mainstream primary school	In special school	Total number of disabled pupils
1994–5	35.6%	64.4%	12,130
1998–9	53.3%	46.7%	15,798
2001–02	57.3%	42.7%	16,358

Source: Department of Education and Science Statistical Reports for 1994–95, 1998–99 and 2001–02

schools. However, while giving a good indication of changing patterns, the figures in the table cannot reflect the full reality. For example, the data on enrolment in mainstream primary schools does not show differences between students in those mainstream schools who were in segregated classes and those who were in mainstream classes. Other research evidence suggests that there is a growing integration into mainstream national schools of students with both physical and learning disabilities, such as Down Syndrome (Egan 2000).

Egan's study (2000) of parents of young people with Down Syndrome also found that the majority wanted access for their children to mainstream schooling. Those parents whose children attended integrated rather than special schools were much happier regarding educational outcomes. As Sailor (1991) argues, students with disabilities in integrated schools can avail of the opportunity to develop the social skills necessary to function productively in the 'real world' after school.

The integration that is currently taking place, however, is relatively ad hoc. Some schools are working positively towards inclusion, while others have taken no action on the matter. In the absence of a comprehensive national policy of mainstreaming and inclusion for all schools, it is inevitable that serious difficulties arise for many parents in placing their children with disabilities in schools (Egan 2000). There is a current difficulty facing some children with disabilities in being enrolled in mainstream primary schools. The enrolment policies of some primary (and post-primary) schools state that in certain circumstances they will postpone the enrolment of a child with special needs until the appropriate supports and resources are put in place by the Department of Education and Science. However, the Department of Education and Science will only put special resources and supports in place for a particular child when that individual is enrolled in a specific school. This situation can result in delays and difficulties for children with disabilities being enrolled.

Even when a student with a disability gains access to a mainstream school, there can be difficulties with genuine inclusion, as schools often lack the support staff and resources required. Integration without appropriate support frequently results in isolation and the dispersal of pupils with disabilities throughout the mainstream system in an unco-ordinated manner (Kenny *et al.* 2000). Furthermore, inclusion without support can lead to a negative rather than a positive educational experience for learners with disabilities (Daly 2001).

Second-level education

The Department of Education and Science lacks comprehensive data on the attendance rates of students with disabilities in post-primary schools.[25] Unlike primary level, where learners with disabilities have recognised entitlements, there are no automatic entitlements for young people in the post-primary sector. A small exploratory study by Kenny *et al.* (2000) suggests that students with disabilities rarely experience formal difficulties in enrolling in their local mainstream post-primary school. However, other evidence would suggest that the nature of the disability may have a significant impact on the likelihood of gaining access. Submissions to the Task Force on Autism (2001) highlighted the current lack of provision and support at post-primary level for autistic young people. Many young people with autism experience great difficulties in gaining access to any kind of post-primary education.

A further issue for students with disabilities, including those with learning difficulties, and students with different ways of learning is their de facto exclusion from many secondary schools on the grounds of curriculum unsuitability. For a range of historical, policy and strategic reasons, many secondary schools in particular (as opposed to

---

[25]While it is possible to get information regarding the numbers of laptops and other equipment given to learners at second level who need specialised support and to get information regarding schools that have had special facilities put in place (such as ramps), enrolment figures given by individual schools to the Department of Education and Science do not specify the precise number of students who have a disability.

community, comprehensive or vocational schools or community colleges) are strongly classical liberal in their curriculum provision. They have neither opted to nor, in some cases, been allowed to offer the technological and practical subjects, such as Wood Technology, Home Economics and Metalwork, or subjects such as Music at junior level. Yet these latter subjects frequently appeal to students whose interests and intelligences are in the bodily kinaesthetic, musical or visual–spatial spheres, rather than in the linguistic or mathematically based disciplines (Gardner 1985).[26] In addition, many schools do not offer the Leaving Certificate Applied or other curriculum options that appeal to students with abilities outside the traditional academic spheres. As secondary schools are in the majority at second level, and as they are often the only realisable or suitable option for certain students, it is incumbent on policy makers at national, regional and local level to address the various issues that currently preclude students with different learning abilities from attending such schools. Moreover, there is a need to re-examine the entire curriculum of second-level education in terms of its suitability for children with different abilities.

A further matter to be addressed at second level, especially where subject options exist, is the assumption at times that students with disabilities do not have the same interests as students who do not have disabilities. Students with physical or sensory disabilities (who are deaf, blind, have cerebral palsy, etc.) are as likely as any other student to have interests in academic subjects. Just because a student has a physical or sensory disability, it must not be assumed that they have learning difficulties as well, although there is evidence that schools sometimes make such assumptions (Duffy 1993).

In an exploratory study conducted by Kenny *et al.* (2000), disabled young people interviewed about their experiences of post-primary schooling spoke of how they wanted to attend and progress in school as normal members of their peer group. Many teachers, school administrators and classmates were kind and supportive, but many others were uncomfortable with their disabilities. As a result, they experienced a sense of being labelled the 'disabled kid'. Duffy's study (1993) on the experiences of disabled girls in integrated settings noted the problems they reported, including the perceived lack of respect some teachers had

---

[26]It goes without saying that technical or musical subjects also appeal to many students who are strong linguistically and mathematically.

for them and the lack of facilitation by the schools of their involvement with extracurricular or social activities, findings that were mirrored in the report by Kenny *et al.* (2000).

Positive curriculum developments at primary and second level

There has been growing recognition at the national level of the inadequacy of existing curricular provision to meet the needs of students with learning disabilities. In 1980 the Department of Education produced curriculum guidelines for teaching pupils with moderate learning disabilities. The Special Education Review Committee (1993) estimated that at second level, between 15 per cent and 18 per cent of students have special learning needs. It recommended that the curricular structures should be examined and a wider range of options made available in order to recognise and facilitate the learning needs of these students. At present, the National Council for Curriculum and Assessment is producing guidelines for schools to enable teachers to mediate existing curriculum objectives and content to meet the needs of various students with learning disabilities. There are three categories: those who have mild, moderate and severe or profound learning disabilities. Primary curriculum guidelines for each of the categories have been completed and work is currently in progress regarding the junior cycle post-primary curriculum. Discussions regarding guidelines for the post-primary senior cycle curriculum are taking place.

Third-level, adult and further education

Given the access and other difficulties that students with disabilities face at primary and second level, it is no surprise that students with disabilities are underrepresented at third level. Although *Learning for Life: White Paper on Adult Education* states that 'between 1,200 and 1,500 students with physical, sensory or learning disabilities participate in third-level education' (Department of Education and Science 2000a: 168), figures provided by the Association for Higher Education Access and Disability (AHEAD) for 1998–9 give a far more conservative estimate (Table 16).

The underrepresentation of people with disabilities at third level can be explained in large part by the absence of an adequate and inclusive education system at primary and second level. The problematic structure regarding special access routes into higher education also needs to be addressed. In research currently being conducted by AHEAD, it is

Table 16. Percentage of third-level students with disabilities

Type of institution	No. of first year students	Proportion of students in each type of institution	No. of students with disabilities in first year	Proportion of students with disabilities in each type of institution	Proportion of first year under-graduate population with disabilities
HEA aided	16,142	43%	171	32%	1.1%
Institute of technology	18,827	50%	317	59%	1.7%
Other institutions	2,543	7%	48	9%	1.9%
Total	**37,512**	**100%**	**536**	**100%**	**1.4%**

Source: Survey on Participation Rates of and Provision for Students with Disabilities in Higher Education for the Academic Year 1998/99, Dublin: Higher Education Authority 2004

emerging that few schools or career guidance teachers working with students with disabilities, and few disabled students themselves, have adequate knowledge of the different routes to higher education.

The majority of third-level colleges now have access officers in place with responsibility for students with disabilities. In addition, the majority of third-level colleges provide some supports and resources for disabled students (Callaghan 2001). The most frequently reported facilities were those enabling the mobility impaired to access buildings, namely providing ramps and altering entrances for wheelchair users. Other more specialised supports, such as Braille services or special facilities for the hearing impaired, were less frequently available. Even when supports are in place, they can be slow and inadequate and may not meet the needs of disabled learners. A previous edition of AHEAD's handbook (1997) also noted that, at the time it was written, only 11 per cent of the fifty-one colleges surveyed were running workshops for staff regarding the requirements of students with disabilities.

The Fund for Students with Disabilities assists third-level students who have special needs. Grants are provided for the purchase of special equipment, special materials, technological aids, targeted transport services and sign language assistance or interpreters. There are standard amounts payable from the fund for specific services. The fund amounted to €3.7 million in 2002 and over 1,000 students were approved for funding (Department of Education and Science 2003b).

There is limited information available on the participation of disabled students in further education and training. *Learning for Life: White Paper on Adult Education* states that there is very little data currently available on the participation of various minority groups, including those with disabilities:

> The figure for VTOS [is] 410 [disabled] students. Data are not available on the representation of such groups across other areas of the education sector. No specific arrangements have been made, until recently, within Further Education to cater for this group (Department of Education and Science 2000a: 168).

One of the functions of the National Adult Learning Council is to prioritise research that will document levels of participation by learners with disabilities in different fields of adult and further education. It is also proposed that it will identify and disseminate models of good practice. The White Paper envisages an enhanced vocational guidance and training role for FÁS to support trainees with disabilities (Department of Education and Science 2000a).

9.3 Diversity recognition issues

While the integration of learners with disabilities into mainstream educational settings is becoming more commonplace, research on inclusion within an Irish context has been limited to date. Apart from a small number of studies examining the experiences of learners with disabilities in integrated settings (e.g. Duffy 1993; O'Keefe 1997; Kitchin and Mulcahy 1999; Kenny *et al.* 2000) and data available from submissions to the Commission on the Status of People with Disabilities (1996) and Task Force on Autism (2001), we know little about the educational experiences of those with disabilities in either mainstream or segregated settings. What the studies do demonstrate is that even if disabled learners successfully gain admission to a school (or indeed, to a third-level college or place of training or further education), they face other difficulties. These have to do with a lack of respect and recognition for them as persons, inadequate institutional facilitation of their needs and, in some cases, systemic failure to recognise their disability and specific needs arising from it. These difficulties were recognised by the Action Group on Access to Third Level (2001).

It is important to recognise that an individual and tragic view of disability has tended to dominate 'both social interactions and social policies' (Oliver 1990). Disabled people have been commonly characterised as 'pitiable', 'pathetic', 'invalid', 'helpless' and 'dependent' (Hevey 1993). In the research domain, disability has been defined in terms of functional deficiencies, and disabled people's views on their own situation and experience have been largely ignored (Oliver 1990). Influenced by these disabling images, societal attitudes can represent the greatest obstacle to the full inclusion of disabled people in the community (Forest 1991).

A study investigating attitudes towards minorities among young people in mainstream education found that the prevailing attitude towards people with disabilities was one of pity (Lodge and Lynch 2001). However, young people who had come to know their disabled peers personally were less likely to define a person by their disability or to regard the person as someone to be pitied (ibid.). Shevlin and O'Moore (1999) argue that the attitudes of young students towards their disabled peers are crucial in making the integration process a successful one. They also found that young people can feel distant from and uneasy around peers with disabilities, particularly when those peers are intellectually disabled. Following prolonged involvement with profoundly intellectually disabled young people, a group of adolescents from a mainstream school became more comfortable with their disabled counterparts. By facilitating this interaction, the mainstream school that the able-bodied young people attended was fostering inclusion and the development of respect for and recognition of different abilities. Mason (1990) argues that schools need to actively challenge attitudes of able-bodyism and able-mindedness that pervade our society.

Teachers' attitudes towards students with disabilities also have a significant impact on educational experience. Kenny *et al.* (2000) note how some of the teachers of the disabled young people involved in their research were respectful and empowering. They were helpful to them and recognised the impact of their disabilities, but also communicated high expectations to them. However, others operated out of a sense of pity for the disabled student and, as a result, did not encourage these students to achieve to the same extent as their able-bodied peers. Still others failed to understand the young person's specific needs and overlooked the genuine difficulties they encountered in school. Butler and Shevlin (2001) have observed that many teachers lack a real understanding of and comfort with the needs of disabled students. Often, they feel genuine concern about their own ability to cope with a disabled learner due in part to the lack of appropriate training that they have received. As was the case with the attitudes of students towards disabled peers, teachers who had experienced working with learners who have disabilities were much more likely to be comfortable with disabled students.

Mukherjee *et al.* (2000) point out that teachers need to have a full understanding of the implications of particular impairments for teaching and learning if they are to inform other students or support students with impairments. The Task Force on Autism (2001) has made similar observations with respect to the education of students with Autistic Syndrome Disorder; up-to-date books and other sources of information on autism are essential guides for teachers and other school personnel. Information helps to dispel the teachers' own fears and it assists them in supporting and providing for the needs of the particular learners. The Task Force on Dyslexia (2001) observed that teachers often failed either to identify or fully recognise a learner's disability or had an inadequate understanding of it.

9.4 Harassment

As was already noted, there is little available research on the experiences of learners with disabilities at any level of education. Consequently we know little about the ways in which people with disabilities experience harassment in schools and colleges or to what extent they do. What has been frequently observed or reported, as was discussed above, is a lack of recognition or respect by both teachers and peers for the disabled individual as a person. The Task Force on Autism (2001) made reference to submissions made by parents of young people with disabilities such as Asperger Syndrome and High Functioning Autism who are either attending or may be enrolled in mainstream schools. Among the primary concerns expressed by parents were either the fears that their child would be subject to bullying and exclusion or actual reports of such peer rejection taking place. There is an onus on educational institutions to proactively tackle lack of awareness around the facts relating to particular disabilities and, in particular, to inform members of the school community about different abilities and disabilities. It is vital that a school's antibullying policy should take account of the need to develop respect for students (or other members of the school community, including teachers and parents) who have disabilities.

9.5 Employment equality issues

There is no public record of the proportion of teachers or education practitioners with disabilities and there is no study of the experience of disabled people in education employment. Therefore it is difficult to draw any clear conclusions about the experience of disabled people in this field. The lack of information about the employment conditions of disabled people is not confined to education, however. Kitchin and Mulcahy (1999) found that data on the employment of disabled people was largely unobtainable in Ireland.

What we do know, however, is that access to employment in primary or post-primary schools requires a degree and other third-level qualification, something few disabled people have acquired. Even where disabled people are qualified for employment, there is evidence that there are many invisible barriers, not least of which are the widespread public discourses of vulnerability and pathos surrounding disability. The ideology of vulnerability creates a perception that disabled people may be a burden rather than an asset to an employer, thereby depressing their employment chances (Kenny *et al.* 2000). Proof that disabled people find it difficult to enter employment is provided in the 1999 FÁS survey of training outcomes for disabled people in Ireland. It found that their chances of getting employment that year were much lower than in former years. Kenny *et al.* (2000) found that even well-educated disabled young people were not optimistic about their employment chances at any level of the labour market.

9.6 Good practice initiatives

- The Education Act 1998 provides a statutory basis for policy and practice in relation to all education provision (Kenny *et al.* 2000). One of the functions of the Minister for Education and Science, as outlined by the Act, is to ensure that each person be provided with an appropriate quality and level of education to meet their needs and abilities. The Act repeatedly makes clear that education users include those with a disability or special educational needs. It defines 'support services' for disabled students in a broad manner as comprising assessment, psychological services, guidance and counselling services, adaptations to the built environment, transport, provision for formal education outside schools and supports for specific pedagogic processes.

• Specialised school placement and support provision for disabled students depends on an assessment of needs. The Department of Education and Science has established a National Educational Psychology Service to improve the assessment procedures. About 130 psychologists have been employed within this service to address the needs of just under 800,000 students in primary and second-level schools. Special schools are still dealt with by the Department of Health and Children's psychological service and by services provided within the voluntary sector.

• There has also been some development in the appointment of specialist personnel for disabled students: in 1993, 8 per cent of primary teachers were in 'special' posts, established to address remedial, special class, disadvantaged (the Breaking the Cycle programme) and home–school liaison needs (Special Education Review Committee 1993). About half the disabled pupils in the 'ordinary classes' availed of the services of a specialist teacher, usually a remedial teacher. The remainder received no additional support beyond what the class teacher or school could provide. Since 1994 there has been a substantial increase in the number of specialist teachers appointed to support disabled pupils in the ordinary classes. As data on specialised teachers is not disaggregated from data on total teacher numbers, it is not possible to assess the precise number of new specialist teachers appointed since 1994.

• The Department of Education and Science has recently introduced a scheme for employment of special needs assistants. Provision for support personnel is far greater at primary level than at second and third levels.

• The Department of Education and Science has a grants scheme to fund assistive technology provision at second level, to which a principal or parents can apply. A maximum grant of €3,809.21 (£3,000) per student is paid to the school for purchase of designated equipment. The assistive technology belongs to the school and the student has use of it only while enrolled there. Grants are also available to enable children in primary schools to have access to assistive technology, but these are granted on an individual basis. At third level, procedures similar to those at second level operate, so the disabled student applies again for such supports on enrolment in college. Timing of payment is problematic, however – approved grants in third level are paid out in February. This means that first year students must manage without supports for the crucial first part of the academic year.

- There are some models of good practice operating at local level within the compulsory sector of the Irish education system. The devolved governance structure of Irish schools leads to difficulties, however, in ascertaining the scope of these initiatives. The lack of a dissemination policy on good practice also means that there is no mechanism whereby schools can learn systematically from each other.

  A few models of good practice are detailed below, as they illustrate the possibilities for developing more inclusive provision for young people with disabilities. However, these examples will remain isolated endeavours unless structural issues are addressed.

  One rural second-level school, with support from the Department of Education and Science, has facilitated the inclusion of young people with hearing difficulties. In the past, these young people would have attended special schools in Dublin and would have had to become boarders. This new approach enables these young people to live at home and to make friends and have a social life in their local community. Supports include sign language interpreters, a learning resource room and a flexible curriculum.

  An urban community school has provided education for a significant number of young people who have Down Syndrome. Reports from parents, teachers and the young people involved have been positive.

- Under the Schools Link Programme, young people from mainstream and special settings have joined together to pursue a common curriculum in arts, physical education and the humanities. In addition, some pupils from special settings have joined their mainstream peers for formal classes in Junior Certificate Science and English.

Chapter 10
Traveller Community

10.1 Introduction and background information

In the Equal Status Acts, the Traveller community is defined as 'the community of people who are commonly called Travellers and who are identified (both by themselves and others) as people with a shared history, culture and traditions including, historically, a nomadic way of life on the island of Ireland' (section 2(1)).

The Traveller community is an indigenous minority that has been a part of Irish society for hundreds of years. Travellers share a nomadic way of life, language, customs, values, traditions and history that mark them as a distinct group.[27]

A question relating to membership of the Irish Traveller community was included for the first time in the 2002 census, and 23,681 Travellers, representing 0.6 per cent of the total population, were enumerated. There were 3,408 Traveller children of four years or younger and 6,503 young people aged five to fourteen. Overall almost two-thirds (62.7 per cent) of the Traveller population was under twenty-five years of age.

Historically, the Traveller community was overlooked in education policy and practice in Ireland. Official concern was first formally expressed in the Commission on Itinerancy's *Report* (1963); this was followed by the Department of Education's report, *Educational Facilities for the Children of Itinerants* (1970). Subsequent reports – the *Report of the Travelling People Review Body* (1983) and the *Report of the Task Force on the Travelling Community* (1995) – and other relevant government policy texts show changes over time in the terminology and conceptual frameworks used to describe Travellers. Reports written during the last two decades have accepted, at least nominally, that the Traveller community has a distinct culture. They do not refer to their way of life as deviant or problematic.

---

[27]This definition is used in the fact sheet 'Irish Travellers' published by Pavee Point on their website (www.paveepoint.ie/fs_irish_a.html).

However, the influence of previous concepts persists in education policy, provision and practice in relation to the Traveller community.

The Commission on Itinerancy's *Report* (1963) operated out of an assimilationist model of integration. It called for conversion and charity on the part of the settled society and settlement and conformity on the part of the Traveller community. The latter were regarded in the report as deviant, destitute drop-outs from a homogeneous Irish population. Education policy focused on the reform of perceived Traveller deviancy and alleviation of destitution, and it promoted a segregated model of provision. There was a focus on hygiene facilities and special curricula emphasising functional literacy, numeracy at primary level and manual skills training at second level.

Subsequent reports, such as the *Report of the Travelling People Review Body* (1983), recognised the right of the Traveller community to retain its own identity and traditions, but regarded Travellers as a subculture of poverty. Education for members of the Traveller community should be compensatory. Low school attainment was blamed on poor home conditions, in particular the lack of permanent accommodation. Traveller children were regarded as needing preschooling as well as special classes and schools. Training centres were perceived as the means of equipping young adults with vocational skills.

It was not until the mid-1990s, with the establishment of the Task Force on Travellers, that Travellers were fully recognised as partners in policy making with respect to their own community. The *Report of the Task Force on the Travelling Community* (1995) recorded the many ways in which education for Traveller children failed to take sufficient account of their culture and lifestyle.

10.2 Presence and participation issues

The Department of Education's *Guidelines for Schools* (1994) states that integrated primary education is the desired education objective for young Traveller children. It also notes that Travellers have a constitutional right to enrol in mainstream schools. As the *Report of the Task Force on the Travelling Community* (1995) points out, however, having a formal right to enrol (see Rule 10 of the *Rules for National Schools* (1965)) did not guarantee Travellers a place. In Ireland, schools exercise considerable autonomy in their selection practices for school entrants. There is evidence that certain schools lay down criteria that can effectively exclude

Travellers, e.g. having the child's name on the waiting list for a long time or the so-called 'first come, first served' principle, while some positively discourage Travellers from entering the school (Flynn 2002). There is also evidence that some schools continue to refuse to enrol Traveller young people on the pretext of being full or by claiming that they cannot provide a suitable education for Traveller children (O'Connell 1998). Through the Visiting Teacher Service for Travellers, the Department of Education and Science supports Travellers in enrolling in schools. The Service also offers advice to Traveller families that experience difficulties about their right to appeal under section 29 of the Education Act 1998 against the decision of a school to refuse to enrol a child. They also offer information on the rights of Traveller children under the Equal Status Acts.

There is no accurate record of Traveller attendance rates in compulsory education or on their performance compared with members of the settled community. Among the reasons for this is the fact that there has not been an agreed ethnic identifier question to date on school data. While there is information on the numbers that enrol, neither the rate of participation nor the levels of attainment are available. The absence of basic research and official statistics on the subject of Traveller participation and attainment is itself an indication of the lack of importance accorded to the education of Travellers.

In 2000–01 there were fifty-two preschools for Traveller children catering for approximately 600 pupils.[28] Other Traveller children attend the Department of Education and Science's Early Start programmes or local preschools provided by community groups. There are approximately 6,000 primary school-age Traveller children enrolled in primary schools[29] (most are enrolled in mainstream classes and a further 125 children are attending the three all-Traveller national schools). However, concerns have been expressed by the Irish National Teachers' Organization (INTO 1995) and others about the attendance levels of Traveller children in primary school. Even though many students are formally enrolled, their attendance is low in many cases. When attendance levels are low and when school drop-out is a common problem, then it is almost inevitable that attainment levels are also low.

Charting Our Education Future: White Paper on Education envisaged that, with supports, all Traveller young people would complete the junior cycle and half would complete the senior cycle of post-primary education by

---

[28]Information accessed at www.paveepoint.ie/fs_educ_a.html.

[29]Estimate made by the National Traveller Education Officer for 1999–2000. Information accessed on www.paveepoint.ie/fs_educ_a.html.

2005 (Department of Education 1995). In 2002 there were 140 post-primary schools with students from the Traveller Community on the roll. The enrolment of Travellers at post-primary level has more than doubled in recent years. In 1997–8 there were 600 Traveller students enrolled in second-level schools. This rose to 1,608 for the school year 2002.[30] There are also three junior education centres[31] catering for young Travellers in the twelve to fifteen age group. In addition, there are twenty-eight senior training centres for young adult Travellers managed by the Vocational Educational Committees (VECs) under the aegis of the Department of Education and Science. These centres, which offer a forty-eight-week training programme, cater for 742 Travellers aged fifteen and over, although the majority of the trainees are aged over eighteen.

The available data suggests that the retention rate for Traveller children of compulsory school age is relatively low. Drop-out rates remain problematic, particularly at the end of the junior cycle and in senior cycle years. Only thirty-eight Traveller young people were attending sixth year in 2001, rising to sixty-three in 2003–04 (Table 17). Fewer than twenty Travellers attended third-level colleges in 2000–01.[32] Many of these were pursuing diploma courses in community care areas. A very small number have enrolled for degree courses. Provision for adult and community-based education began to develop in the 1990s, initiated primarily by Pavee Point.

Table 17. Distribution of Traveller students in mainstream post-primary schools

School year	First year	Second year	Third year	TY*	Fifth year	Sixth year	PLC	Total
2000–01	531	319	183	27	67	38	13	1,178
2001–02	582	397	220	31	86	49	16	1,381
2002–03	650	482	272	26	102	62	14	1,608
2003–04	626	527	341	44	113	63	15	1,729

*Transition year.

Source: Unpublished data supplied by the National Education Officer for Travellers

[30]Information provided by the Social Inclusion Unit, Department of Education and Science and based on estimated figures reported by Visiting Teachers for Travellers.

[31]The curriculum in the Junior Training Centres concentrates on functional literacy and numeracy, religion, physical education, social and personal development and arts and crafts (Kenny 1997).

[32]Information accessed on www.paveepoint.ie/fs_educ_a.html.

Undoubtedly one of the practices that is depressing second-level school attendance is the fact that many Travellers can transfer out of education into paid training at the age of fifteen, which encourages early school leaving. Yet there has been no independent evaluation of the merits of training centres for Traveller students compared with mainstream schools.

One of the reasons for early school leaving cited by young Travellers themselves is their sense of isolation in school, especially if there are few other Traveller students present. They do not feel part of the dominant settled peer group, experiencing themselves as outsiders (Trainees of St Joseph's Training Centre 2000). This sense of being different and outsiders arose particularly because of differences between the lifestyles of Travellers and settled students. The level of family responsibility borne by many young Traveller women, for example, means that their life experiences are very different from that of their settled peers (ibid.). There is also evidence that some Traveller young people and their parents see post-primary schooling in particular as a threat to the maintenance of Traveller culture – they feel they are exposed to lifestyles and values that do not fit easily with a nomadic way of life and established Traveller customs (McDonagh 2000).

There is also a belief that the education system is insufficiently flexible to educate students who are nomadic rather than sedentary. Some Traveller young people have reported a sense of teachers 'giving up on them' because of their nomadic way of life (McDonagh 2000). Students and parents also report that the poor living conditions and lack of facilities also militate against young Travellers' full participation in education (O'Connell 1998). The low or irregular attendance at school by Traveller young people can also be a consequence of the real difficulties Traveller parents face in getting their children enrolled in schools. Even when children are enrolled, there is a general lack of recognition of the specific cultural values of Travellers (O'Connell 1998). The *Guidelines on Traveller Education* (Department of Education and Science 2002d, 2002e) and a series of seminars organised by the Visiting Teacher Service for parents and teachers have sought to address this problem.

The underrepresentation of members of the Traveller community in further education and training and at third level can only be understood in the context of low participation levels within the compulsory sector. As McDonagh (2000) observes, to benefit from most adult and further education courses, literacy skills are essential. Without high levels of literacy and general education attainment, members of the Traveller community are automatically precluded from accessing and succeeding in either further or third-level education. This means, in turn, that most Travellers are excluded from the very professions and occupations that service their own communities, including health, education and accommodation.

10.3 Diversity recognition issues

Traveller culture, values, traditions and history continue to have little visibility within school texts and other learning materials. This invisibility contributes to the sense of isolation and exclusion experienced by Traveller young people within education (McDonagh 2000; Trainees of St Joseph's Training Centre 2000). The *Report of the Task Force on the Travelling Community* (1995) cites the disregard for nomadic traditions in schools' programmes as a significant factor in discouraging Travellers from actively engaging and continuing with schooling.

The *Revised Primary School Curriculum* has a stated commitment to inclusion and the recognition of diversity (Department of Education and Science 1999b). It encourages schools and teachers to develop materials suited to their particular local culture. Programmes such as Civic, Social and Political Education (CSPE) at the junior cycle of post-primary also provide opportunities to examine the cultures, values and traditions of groups such as the Traveller community.

Central to the successful provision of such programmes are teachers' awareness, knowledge and positive attitudes towards various minority groups represented in the school, including members of the Traveller community. *Charting Our Education Future: White Paper on Education* names Travellers as a 'community with deep roots in Irish society...[with] a right to...have its traditions respected' (Department of Education 1995: 26), and it advocates modules on Traveller culture in teacher training and integrated schooling for all. Despite this, it is far from clear how well teachers are prepared to work with specific minority ethnic groups such as Travellers. There are no monitoring procedures to establish if teacher education courses address issues pertaining to Travellers or, indeed, other minorities.

Charting Our Education Future: White Paper on Education (Department of Education 1995) and both of the *Guidelines on Traveller Education* (Department of Education and Science 2002d, 2002e) note the importance of a curriculum *for* Travellers as a mechanism for meeting their particular needs. Meeting the learning needs of Travellers in a culturally sensitive manner addresses only part of the recognition problem, however. Mainstreaming education for all students on Traveller traditions, history, culture and values is also essential to counter the negative attitudes towards the Traveller community that pervade much of Irish society (MacLaughlin 1995; MacGreil 1996).

Part of the problem in relation to realising change in educational attitudes to Travellers stems from the relative exclusion of Travellers from policy making in the educational field. While groups such as Travellers may be occasionally consulted on an ad hoc basis on educational matters, there is no mandatory requirement to consult them. Under the Education Act 1998, consultation on most education matters is confined to a limited group of organisations. The specific groups named for consultative purposes throughout the Act are 'patrons, national associations of parents, recognised school management organisations and recognised trade unions and staff associations representing teachers'. Organisations outside of the immediate education nexus are excluded from having a right to a consultative role. The failure to include minority groups, including the Traveller community, in planning for services such as education is indicative of unintentional institutional racism. This has begun to change through the inclusion of Travellers and Traveller organisations on the Advisory Committee on Traveller Education, although this does not change the question of Traveller participation as a right.

Unless the perspectives and lived realities of minority groups are part of the planning and development process in services such as education, exclusion and misrecognition of minorities cannot be meaningfully challenged. Traveller organisations can make a central contribution to the development of a more intercultural education that is better able to recognise difference (Irish Traveller Movement 2000). Where Traveller parents have become engaged as partners with schools in planning their children's education, positive changes have occurred in the educational experience of parents, children and teachers (McDonagh 2000).

10.4 Harassment

Travellers are among the most marginalised groups in Irish society (O'Connell 1998). They are frequently subject to negative stereotyping, both in terms of the way the group is depicted and regarded and in terms of the way individuals are treated. Examples of racist depictions of the Traveller community can be found in statements made by public figures, including politicians and journalists (MacLaughlin 1995; McVeigh 1995). Fear and prejudice towards Travellers have also been expressed by young people in schools. Even when teachers attempted to introduce alternative perspectives on the Traveller community, these met with active resistance by students (Lynch and Lodge 1999; Lodge and Lynch 2001).

Given the level of publicly expressed prejudice against Travellers, it is not surprising that some Traveller parents believe that their children are more likely to develop positive self-esteem in segregated training centres (McDonagh 2000). They fear that their children will experience bullying and rejection in a mainstream school. Parents who had negative experiences of schooling themselves are especially likely to feel this way (ibid.). One of the interesting points to emerge from discussions with the settled young people about Travellers, however, is that they were less likely to express prejudice and fear against Travellers if they had come to know Travellers personally (Lynch and Lodge 1999).

10.5 Employment equality issues

We do not know of any Traveller teacher working in a compulsory sector school. The nonparticipation of Travellers in professional areas such as teaching is a legacy of relatively poor participation by and provision for Traveller young people in compulsory education, resulting in their lack of access to further and third-level education. Furthermore, the lack of recognition within the education system of Traveller culture and values remains problematic.

During 2000, the Irish Traveller Movement engaged with Mary Immaculate College, Limerick regarding the development of a project aimed at enabling Travellers to participate in teacher education (Irish Traveller Movement 2000). While there has been no specific progress in the meantime, interest in the project remains. In recent years Travellers have begun to gain employment within education support areas. There are a number of Traveller women working as classroom assistants, particularly in the preschool sector. Others work as education development workers (McDonagh 2000) and in other parts of the community and voluntary sector.

10.6 Good practice initiatives

- The National Education Officer for Travellers is responsible for identifying needs and promoting good school policies and practices at preschool, primary and post-primary levels.

- On application by local committees or schools and following assessment of need by the Department of Education and Science, transport provision for Travellers can be grant aided. A transport scheme for Travellers in some primary schools is grant aided; at second level, special transport is funded in certain circumstances.

- Post-primary schools with Travellers on the roll are entitled to apply for additional grant aid, e.g. information technology funding and enhanced capitation grants. They can also apply for additional teaching hours to provide for extra teaching for Traveller students, targeting literacy and numeracy in particular (Department of Education and Science 1999e). This has been the first formal promise of resources to increase Traveller participation at post-primary level. There are currently over 540 resource teachers for Travellers at primary level.

- The Visiting Teacher Service, begun in 1980 as a pilot scheme, now has forty permanent posts. The service is family based and its staff have cross-sectional responsibility at primary and post-primary levels and liaise with preschool providers. The visiting teachers support parents, schools and other agencies in maximising Traveller students' participation and attainment and in promoting antiracist intercultural policies and programmes. Visiting Traveller teachers receive about five days of training per school year, covering needs they identify, such as facilitation skills and strategies for promoting antiracism and intercultural policy and programmes for schools. The Visiting Teacher Service is still developing, and discussions have begun with a view to developing its management structures nationally.

- The Advisory Committee on Traveller Education in the Department of Education and Science includes Traveller representatives from Pavee Point, the Irish Traveller Movement and the National Traveller Women's Forum. The *Report of the Task Force on the Travelling Community* (1995) recommended that a dedicated Traveller Unit be established within the Department of Education. This recommendation has not been implemented. However, an internal Co-ordinating Committee was established in 1996 within the Department of Education. This was complemented by the Advisory Committee, with Traveller representatives, in 1998.

- Traveller representatives have been involved in the delivery of in-career development programmes on issues of interculturalism and Traveller education for teachers. Two national seminars organised by the National Education Officer for Travellers and the Visiting Teacher Service in 1997 (on primary education) and 1999 (on post-primary education) included presentations from Traveller parents and young people.

- As noted in Chapter 8 on the race ground, the National Council for Curriculum and Assessment has appointed officers to develop guidelines on intercultural education.

- Within the university sector, a Certificate Programme in Equality Studies (with a focus on primary health care for Travellers) has been developed as a joint initiative between Traveller groups and University College Dublin with the support of the Eastern Regional Health Authority.

- The Department of Education and Science produced two sets of guidelines on Traveller Education, one dealing with primary education and one dealing with post-primary education, in 2002. Both documents offer guidelines on school planning for the inclusion and retention of students from the Traveller community and address the need to develop curricula that recognise Traveller culture.

- Higher Education Authority-designated universities are engaged in initiatives which include antiracism and intercultural research, awareness raising and training. They are also extending existing initiatives to support learners to include members of the Traveller community.

Chapter 11

Conclusion –
Strategies for Change

11.1 Introduction

Education consists of an enormously complex and diverse set of social institutions in which over one million people participate as students and in which some 40,000 people are employed. Realising change in education is therefore a diverse and challenging task. However, all research undertaken on realising change in education recognises that if change is to occur, the stakeholders within it need to own it and promote it. Top-down or outside-in solutions by and large have a temporary and superficial effect. Given the diversity of the interests in education and their relative autonomy from other social actors, working with them for change represents a considerable challenge.

Strategies for change will need to encompass:

- change of culture and attitudes of the way we think about and relate to people who are different from us

- change in organisational practices to promote and achieve equality

- change in practices and processes that shape legislation, economic relations, political relations, cultural relations and affective relations.

The strategies that are discussed below involve a combination of actions to realise change across these three fields. While some of the changes proposed are relatively easy to implement, others will require sustained analysis and action over many years. Each one is important if we are to create a truly inclusive education system. Given that many inegalitarian assumptions are deeply embedded in our ways of thinking and are encoded in our laws, policies and practices in ways that silence discussion about their very existence, the barriers to such change cannot be underestimated.

The strategies for change are set out in relation to a number of areas:

- informing education partners about equality

- developing good equality practices

- equality in national educational planning.

Some of the suggestions for change identify specific types of educational institutions, while others should be taken up by educational institutions at all levels. For clarity, we use 'educational institutions' to mean educational institutions at all levels from preschool services through schools, and institutions of adult, community, further and higher education.

11.2 Informing education partners about equality

Under the Education Act 1998, a number of key partners (in addition to the Minister and staff of the Department of Education and Science) are identified as playing a central role in education policy as it relates to schools. These include teacher unions, national parents' associations, school management bodies and school patrons (including the Vocational Education Committees). A further set of educators exists in the further, higher and adult and community education sectors. Their specific equality responsibilities are set out in the relevant legislation governing their operations. In addition, a number of statutory bodies and support agencies have important roles. Examples of these are the National Council for Curriculum and Assessment, the National Educational Welfare Board, the Higher Education Authority and the agencies and support services of the Department of Education and Science in areas such as school development planning, the curriculum, guidance, etc. Students are also key partners in their own education. If equality-related change is to be promoted in education, each of the partners needs to be involved in the project.

Information on equality legislation

Part of the task of further improving equality practice in educational institutions is disseminating information about the implications of the equality legislation for educational practice. There is limited awareness among those engaged in education across all levels regarding the impact and relevance of the equality legislation (in particular the Equal Status Acts). This lack of knowledge needs to be addressed through the dissemination of information to all of the educational partners. **In-service training should be provided for teachers, principals, lecturers, tutors and management authorities about the equality legislation.** Management authorities include those who serve on school boards of management and members of governing bodies in institutions of higher education, as well as staff in all educational institutions who have management roles. Those in statutory bodies and support agencies need to be informed about both their own responsibilities and those of the 'front-line' service providers with whom they work. Students and their parents need to be given information about the rights they (or their children) have and how these rights can be enforced. They also need to be informed of duties they (or their children) have in respect of others.

Teachers and other partners
Educators will need to be supported to further develop their knowledge and capacity in relation to equality and how inequality in education can be combated. The education faculties and departments in universities and the colleges of education are important in this context, as is the Teaching Council with its role in establishing standards for programmes of teacher education and training, including the continuing training and professional development of teachers. **A plan for integrating education about and for equality into the teacher education curriculum should be developed.** One element of this could be an assessment of each teacher's equality practices in the classroom as part of the appraisal of his or her preservice teaching practice. (This procedure already operates in a number of teacher education departments in the UK.) **At further and higher education levels, the objective should be to have equality modules in induction courses for new lecturers and in-service opportunities for existing lecturers.** With preparatory courses being increasingly compulsory for new academic staff in the colleges of higher education, there is a good opportunity to enhance equality practice in that field.

Other key stakeholders in education, including patrons, unions, management bodies, parents, students, statutory bodies and support services, all need to have ownership of education about and for equality. Supporting such wide-ranging groups in this is a more difficult task, not least because of the different roles of these different education partners.

However, it is important to build the capacity of these bodies in relation to equality issues given the central role they play in equality in education.

Students

Students also need education about and for equality. One of the most significant omissions in Irish education is the absence of a strong intellectual tradition focused on equality, human rights and social justice. There is a need for both mainstreaming education about equality across all subjects and targeting particular subjects to include such a focus. Without programmes in educational institutions directly focused on equality, it will be very difficult to create an inclusive environment for different groups.

Therefore, it is recommended that education about equality becomes more systematic in educational institutions. Equality principles need to inform all programmes taught in schools, regardless of whether there are members of groups from the nine grounds named in the equality legislation on the roll.

Possibilities for action include building on equality-related modules and perspectives within existing subjects (most obviously within Civic, Social and Political Education (CSPE) in schools) and developing a strong element on equality and diversity into the proposed new senior cycle course on social and political education in schools. The further development of curricular materials needs to be undertaken in collaboration with members of organisations representing the nine grounds. In the context of the affective domain, there is a need for all children to learn about caring work as part of their formal education, as everyone has care responsibilities at some stage in their life.

The promotion of equality-related education within further, higher, adult and community education is also important.

11.3 Developing good equality practices

Ensuring educational achievements across a diverse range of pupils and students and creating a climate within educational institutions that is welcoming of students and staff from nontraditional background, of both boys and girls, of men and women and of those who belong to minority groups cannot happen without concerted action on the part of the educational bodies involved. Educational institutions need to proactively promote equality and actively combat discrimination. Promoting antidiscrimination measures will boost inclusiveness, while action to promote inclusion will create an environment that is hostile to discrimination. **To bring about real change, educational institutions should devise equality action plans (not just write policies) with definite targets, measurable objectives and specific timescales as well as having clear reporting mechanisms and implementation strategies.**[33] Such strategies will need to address questions of who delivers education, the visibility and inclusion of diverse groups across the nine equality grounds in the education system – among both educators and students – and patterns of seniority and achievement. Particular issues in these regards arise in the gender, disability, sexual orientation, race and Traveller grounds. **A positive duty should be established in the equality legislation requiring the preparation of these equality action plans.** This could draw from the experience of similar provisions in race relations legislation in Great Britain.

Integrating equality into strategic plans
Education legislation has identified equality as an important governing principle in the life of both schools and third-level institutions. Under the Education Act 1998 schools are required in their school plans to state the objectives of the school relating to equality of access and participation and to identify the measures that the school proposes to take to achieve these equality objectives. Under the Universities Act 1997 each university is required to prepare and implement policies on equality in all its activities. The institutes of technology are also required to have regard to equality in performing their functions.

Educational institutions should be equipped to develop and implement informed equality policies and plans. This includes access to information, training and resources. The focus for these should cover nondiscrimination, reasonable accommodation and positive action as allowed under the equality legislation.

Equality plans for educational institutions and indicators of achievement should be drawn up by the educational institutions in co-operation with the education partners, local communities (and

---

[33]Several colleges have equality policies at present. However, it is often unclear how these are implemented or monitored. There is no external monitoring or sanctions for schools and colleges whose policies are ineffectual. The absence of visible change in institutional practices and outcomes creates deep cynicism and makes the achievement of equality seem impossible.

regional and national organisations in the case of institutions of education that have regional or national remits) and representatives of those who experience inequality. This should be an integrated part of the school planning process or the development of the equality policies.

Clear equality objectives are required in these plans and indicators of progress are needed. Monitoring by both internal and external bodies of equality policies and plans of educational institutions at all levels is important, as well as monitoring their implementation.

It will not be possible to implement any of the above actions without proper resources, thus **staff should be specifically designated to undertake equality work.** This would have a particular relevance in higher education institutions.[34] Equality planning work needs to be recognised for promotional purposes for staff in schools.

Admission and enrolment policies
Under the Education Act 1998 all schools are required to formulate and publish an enrolment policy. **This policy and the equivalent policies in other education institutions should ensure that no one is denied access to a place on the basis of discrimination on any of the nine grounds in the equality legislation (unless it is an exemption specifically allowed for by law).**

Admission policies for education institutions at all levels have a role in promoting equality. **Educational institutions should identify initiatives in their admission policies to make reasonable accommodation for people with disabilities and should identify positive action measures to address disadvantage and meet special needs (including special needs other than special educational needs) for students across the nine grounds.** For those students who need supports, educational institutions should ensure that the resources are made available to make admission of these students a reality.

Particular issues in the context of transfer and progression in further and higher education sectors have been highlighted by the National Qualifications Authority of Ireland (NQAI). These sectors are of particular relevance to those learners who had limited access to education and training awards in the past. Such learners include those with limited levels

---

[34]Queen's University Belfast has established a special gender equality unit to promote equality for women and men. This is in addition to another unit that has responsibility for implementing the Fair Employment legislation.

of basic education, mature learners, older learners, people with disabilities, members of the Traveller community or other minority ethnic groups and refugees. (The NQAI also drew attention to learners who are unemployed or not in the labour force, workers in unskilled or low-skilled occupations and those living in remote or isolated locations.) **Admission policies in the further and higher education institutions should take account of the particular situation of these learners.**

The Education Act 1998 (in section 29) establishes the right of appeal against a school decision in the event of a refusal to enrol or to expel from a school. It is important that members of the appeal boards established under section 29 of the Education Act are aware of and sensitive to the rights of groups named in the equality legislation.

The Department of Education and Science should issue clear guidelines on promoting equality and combating discrimination in the selection of students. The Department needs to monitor their operation and impose sanctions where they are not being implemented.

Accommodating diversity

The accommodation of diversity presents a range of challenges for education practice. Accommodating diversity is about taking account of the practical implications of difference among students and staff across the nine grounds covered by the equality legislation.

The content of the curriculum, the materials used and the teaching methodologies should take account of differences across the nine grounds named in the equality legislation. The curriculum should be assessed for what it communicates and teaches about groups across all of the nine grounds. Stereotyping, inaccurate messages and absences of messages about groups across the nine grounds need to be identified and rectified. This applies not only to explicit statements, but also to implicit messages, such as visual images in textbooks. **The accessibility of the curriculum and the materials used, both for those with disabilities and for other groups, should be assessed.** This work needs to be done in partnership with organisations representing those who experience inequality. Any decision regarding the nature and development of syllabi and materials can only be successfully implemented when the views of all stakeholders are taken into account.

A particular challenge in accommodating diversity that will grow in significance is the changing religious profile of Irish society. Two issues will need to be addressed. The first of these arises because it is likely that existing denominational schools will have increasing numbers of students who are not of the denomination of the school's patron. **As the state makes provision for education through its support for denominational schools, the Department of Education and Science should ensure that the rights of those who are not of the particular religious belief of the school are respected.** This will need to go beyond respecting the right not to be given teaching in a different religion (for example, through withdrawal during religious instruction) to ensuring that those who are of a different religion (or none) are fully equal and appropriately accommodated for in the life of the school.

The second challenge that arises with the changing religious profile of Irish society is the growth in demand for multidenominational education. **The Department of Education and Science should change its procedures for the preparation of applications for new schools and the supports it provides in the initial years before capital funding for permanent premises is provided to ensure that multidenominational schools are not at a disadvantage compared with religious-run patron bodies.**

Training, recruitment and staffing practices

A number of groups across the nine grounds do not participate equally in delivering education or are invisible. **Colleges and faculties of education and teacher education should be proactive in encouraging people with disabilities, Black and minority ethnic people (including Travellers), both genders and lesbian, gay and bisexual people into the teaching profession in Ireland.**

Education institutions at all levels should ensure their recruitment and promotion processes and practices do not contribute to imbalances that currently exist on the gender, disability, age, race, Traveller and sexual orientation grounds and modify them where necessary. Education institutions at all levels should develop planned and systematic approaches to promoting equality across all nine grounds in the employment of staff. Recruitment and promotion processes need to be assessed for any barriers they might present to diversity among staff at all levels. Employment equality policies, equality and diversity training for staff and employment equality action plans are the key elements of a planned and systematic approach.

109

Harassment and sexual harassment

Antibullying guidelines for schools have been formulated and disseminated by the Department of Education and Science. Under the Education (Welfare) Act 2000, the National Educational Welfare Board may prepare guidelines for schools on their codes of behaviour, and the Board is planning to prepare such guidelines. These guidelines should take account of the prohibitions in the Equal Status Acts of harassment across the nine grounds and of sexual harassment.

The code of behaviour that schools are required to develop under the Education (Welfare) Act 2000 should: explicitly name the nine grounds in the equality legislation and prohibit harassment and sexual harassment on these nine grounds; set out procedures for dealing with any such incident that might arise; require behaviour that respects diversity across the nine grounds; and identify initiatives to build a harassment-free environment in schools.

School policies for preventing and combating harassment and sexual harassment should take account of the difficulties students (and teachers) can experience in schools. These difficulties may arise because they belong to a minority group or because of their gender. Schools should be encouraged and assisted in taking a proactive approach to address the negative and fearful attitudes that can create a context for bullying behaviour or harassment towards minorities and on the gender ground.

Education providers that are not covered by the Education (Welfare) Act 2000 should also adapt their codes of conduct or behaviour and their related practices and policies to ensure that they name as prohibited any harassment that is illegal under the equality legislation and that they take action in relation to such harassment or sexual harassment if it does occur.

Disseminating good practice

As models of good practice develop, there is a need to ensure that information about such practices is widely disseminated. This would encourage other schools and educational providers to take similar initiatives. **Such dissemination should be facilitated through initiatives such as developing a database on models of good equality practice with contact information, etc.** A website on models of good practice could be developed. Information could also be disseminated about such practices by organising an annual forum on 'Models of Good Practice' to which educators and education partners are invited.

Supporting and enforcing standards

Legislation governing schools and other education institutions places a number of duties on these bodies in respect of their policies. These include the requirement of schools to have school development plans, codes of behaviour and admission policies, and of universities to have strategic development plans and equality policies.

At school level, bodies such as the National Educational Welfare Board and the two School Development Planning support services have roles in supporting schools to meet their obligations. At third level, this function, to the extent that it exists, lies with the Higher Education Authority. Two bodies have roles in reviewing compliance with the legislative requirements and for evaluating the standards attained, both in the content of the written policies and in their implementation: the Department's Inspectorate in relation to schools and the Higher Education Authority in relation to institutions in the higher education sector.

The Department of Education and Science should ensure that all agencies under its aegis that have a role in supporting schools – including the Inspectorate, the School Development Planning support services, the National Education Psychological Service and the National Educational Welfare Board – promote equality across the nine grounds in all of their work with schools. The existing guidelines, supports, awareness raising and training should be developed to further assist schools in identifying and eliminating policies that can result in discrimination, including harassment and sexual harassment, and in identifying and implementing policies that support inclusion and equality.

The two School Development Planning support services should further develop their resources to assist schools in identifying and undertaking positive action designed to achieve full equality in practice for those covered by the equality legislation. The purpose of these resources should include assisting schools in identifying meaningful equality objectives and practical steps to achieve full equality in practice.

The National Educational Welfare Board should prepare guidelines for schools on drafting codes of behaviour. These guidelines should state that all nine grounds should be named in the code of behaviour, that codes should state that harassment and sexual harassment will not be tolerated and that behaviour that respects diversity across these grounds is required. The guidelines should set out that the code should identify the positive steps the institution will take to prevent harassment and sexual harassment from happening and the steps that will be taken if either does occur.

The Higher Education Authority should develop similar supports for institutions within its remit.

The Inspectorate has developed a set of tools for the evaluation of schools that includes assessments of these requirements. These include self-evaluation tools (Department of Education and Science 2003c, 2003d) and the templates it uses in conducting whole school evaluations in primary schools.

The Inspectorate should further develop its evaluation mechanisms and tools to enable an assessment to be made of the equality focus in admission policies, school plans and the code of behaviour.

The Higher Education Authority should develop standards and evaluation tools in relation to the inclusion of an equality focus across the nine grounds in equality policies and in strategic development plans in the education institutions within its remit.

Both the Higher Education Authority and the Inspectorate should identify appropriate sanctions that can be applied to education institutions that fail to meet these duties.

11.4 Equality in national educational planning

A core challenge for national policymakers will be to work with the key stakeholders in education in establishing strategies and action plans for the promotion of equality across all education sectors.

Strategy

The announcement by the Minister for Education and Science in April 2003 of his intention to create a new vision for education and to engage in a national consultative process in developing this provides an important opportunity for the issue of equality in education to be further developed. **Any such review should involve the development of a national strategy for equality in education that is based on the principle of creating inclusive schools and colleges.**

Structure

The Department of Education and Science should expand the remit of its Gender Equality Unit to include a focus on all grounds covered by equality legislation and ensure an input to the work of the unit from organisations representing those who experience inequality across the nine grounds.

Involvement in educational planning and decision making

Irish education has adopted a partnership approach in policy making, involving consultation between the Department of Education and Science and other partners identified in the Education Act 1998. At present this model of consultation is limited in that it does not require consultation with or participation by organisations representing women (a majority group) and others who experience inequality across the nine grounds. **Representatives of groups across the nine grounds named in the equality legislation should be involved in the development of educational policy, planning and service delivery, particularly with regard to educational issues that directly concern them.**

Addressing the information deficit

Planning for equality in education must be based on accurate information. However, there is a lack of substantive, accurate data about the educational experiences of those who experience inequality under several of the nine grounds named in the equality legislation. There is a need to actively address this information deficit.

Statistical data relating to teachers, lecturers and students is collected annually by the Statistics Branch of the Department of Education and Science. While this does include valuable data, especially on gender, there is a lack of data on others who experience inequality across the nine grounds. There is also a lack of comprehensive national data on those participating in community and adult education programmes. Initiatives to address data gaps should take account of the work of the National Statistics Board's Steering Group on Social and Equality Statistics. **In particular, the Department of Education and Science should establish a Data Strategy Committee, as recommended by the National Statistics Board (2004), and use it to design and deliver a data strategy that enables policies, practices and outcomes in education to be adequately assessed from an equality perspective.**

Research

Irish research examining the experiences of the education system by certain groups is limited. This needs to be addressed. A number of areas for further research can be identified across a range of grounds. **The Department of Education and Science should develop and fund a research strategy to support a focus on equality in education.** This could focus on employment, educational experiences and the development of an equality focus in particular areas of provision.

Resources

Realising educational outcomes for a diversity of students and promoting a culture in education that is respectful of difference, both in theory and in practice, requires investment. Inadequate resourcing of policies, programmes and initiatives that are designed to achieve equality in education can lead to disillusionment and frustration with the equality project itself. **If equality in education is to be promoted in a substantive manner, resources should be invested in achieving it.** This is particularly important when it comes to resourcing schools, colleges and the informal sector to develop equality action plans and to implement them successfully.

Resources should be invested in proactively removing the barriers experienced by some groups in accessing educational institutions and in securing a presence and participation in education for students across all nine grounds.

In addition to the provision of resources to institutions, there is a need for adequate supports to enable those who experience inequality to avail of the opportunities that exist. A number of grounds in the equality legislation have barriers associated with them and these need to be addressed. Examples include:

- child care and relief care for other dependents underpins access to education for all

- many forms of current provision of financial assistance for participation in education and training are accessed on the basis of household incomes rather than on the income of the particular individual concerned

- the lack of adequate financial support for mature learners who wish to participate in education programmes means that many are indirectly excluded by lack of finance

- in order to be able to participate fully in education, those who have disabilities need to be provided with adequate back-up facilities and resources, such as assistive technology, personal assistants, accessible learning material, etc.

Bibliography

Action Group on Access to Third Level (2001), *Report of the Action Group on Access to Third Level,* Dublin: Department of Education and Science.

AHEAD (1997), *Accessing Third Level Education in Ireland: A Handbook for Students with Disabilities,* Dublin: AHEAD.

APVSCC (1998), *National Survey of Student Absenteeism in VEC Second-Level Schools,* Tralee: APVSCC.

Archer, P. (2001), 'Public Spending on Education, Inequality and Poverty', in S. Cantillon, C. Corrigan, P. Kirby and J. O'Flynn (eds.), *Rich and Poor: Perspectives on Tackling Inequality in Ireland,* Dublin: Oak Tree Press in association with Combat Poverty Agency.

Arnot, M., Gray, J., James, M. and Ruddock, J. (1998), *Recent Research on Gender and Educational Performance,* London: Stationery Office for OFSTED.

Bailey, I. and Coleman, U. (1998), *Access and Participation in Adult Literacy Schemes,* Dublin: Aontas.

Barron, M. (1999), 'Lesbian, Gay and Bisexual Experiences of School', Maynooth: unpublished thesis in youth studies, National University of Ireland, Maynooth.

Blossfeld, H.P. and Shavit, Y. (1993), 'Persisting Barriers in Educational Opportunities in Thirteen Countries', in Y. Shavit and H.P. Blossfeld (eds.), *Persistent Inequality: Changing Educational Attainments in Thirteen Countries,* Oxford: Westview Press.

Boldt, S. (1998), *Age and Opportunity. The Educational Needs of People Aged 55 and Over: A Study in the Midland and Western Health Board Regions,* Dublin: Marino Institute of Education.

Boucher, G.W. (1998), *The Irish are Friendly, But…: A Report on Racism and International Students in Ireland,* Dublin: Irish Council for Overseas Students.

Bourke, J. (1998), 'Getting it Right for the Child', *Irish Times Education and Living Supplement,* 21 April 1998.

Bowen, K. (1983), *Protestants in a Catholic State: Ireland's Privileged Minority,* Dublin: Gill & Macmillan.

Broderick, G. (2000), 'Pulling Down the Shutters: The Asylum System in Ireland in the 1990s', Dublin: unpublished thesis in equality studies, University College Dublin.

Butler, S. and Shevlin, M. (2001), 'Creating an Inclusive School: The Influence of Teacher Attitudes', *Irish Educational Studies,* vol. 20, pp.125–38.

Byrne, A. (1997), 'Single Women in Ireland: A Re-examination of the Sociological Evidence', in A. Byrne and M. Leonard (eds.), *Women and Irish Society: A Sociological Reader,* Belfast: Beyond the Pale Publications.

Caird, D. (1985), 'Protestantism and National Identity', in J. McLoone (ed.), *Being Protestant in Ireland: Papers Presented at the 32nd Annual Summer School of the Social Study Conference,* Galway: Social Study Conference and Dublin: Co-operation North.

Callaghan, P., with revisions by C. McGrath and M. Scanlan (2001), *Accessing Third Level in Ireland: A Handbook for Students with Disabilities and Learning Difficulties,* 4th ed., Dublin: AHEAD.

Clancy, P. (1982), *Participation in Higher Education,* Dublin: Higher Education Authority.

Clancy, P. (1988), *Who Goes to College?,* Dublin: Higher Education Authority.

Clancy, P. (1995), *Access to College: Patterns of Continuity and Change,* Dublin: Higher Education Authority.

Clancy, P. (1999), 'Education Policy', in S. Quin, P. Kennedy, A. O'Donnell and G. Kiely (eds.), *Contemporary Irish Social Policy,* Dublin: UCD Press.

Clancy, P. (2002), *College Entry in Focus: A Fourth National Survey of Access to Higher Education,* Dublin: Higher Education Authority.

Clancy, P. and Benson, C. (1979), *Higher Education in Dublin: A Study of Some Emerging Needs,* Dublin: Higher Education Authority.

Clancy, P. and Wall, J. (2000), *Social Backgrounds of Higher Education Entrants,* Dublin: Higher Education Authority.

Clarke, D. (1998), 'Education, The State and Sectarian Schools', in T. Murphy and P. Twomey (eds.), *Ireland's Evolving Constitution, 1937–1997: Collected Essays,* Oxford: Hart Publishing.

Cleary, A., Nic Ghiolla Phadraig, M. and Quin, S. (2001), 'Introduction', in A. Cleary, M. Nic Ghiolla Phadraig and S. Quin (eds.), *Understanding Children Volume 1: State, Education and Economy,* Cork: Oak Tree Press.

Commission on Itinerancy (1963), *Report,* Dublin: Stationery Office.

Commission on the Family (1998), *Strengthening Families for Life. Final Report of the Commission on the Family to the Minister for Social, Community and Family Affairs,* Dublin: Stationery Office.

Commission on the Status of People with Disabilities (1996), *A Strategy for Equality,* Dublin: Stationery Office.

Connell, R.W. (1993), *Schools and Social Justice,* Philadelphia: Temple University Press.

Cooke, J. (1997), *Marley Grange Multi-denominational School Challenge 1973–1978,* Dublin: J. Cooke.

Coolahan, J. (1981), *Irish Education: Its History and Structure,* Dublin: Institute of Public Administration.

Coyle, C. (1997), *Relationships and Sexuality Education: Resources Guide,* Dublin: Marino Institute of Education.

CPSMA (2000), *Management Board Members' Handbook* (Revised 2000), Dublin: Catholic Primary School Management Association.

CPSMA (2001), *Solas, Newsletter of the CPSMA Issued to National Schools under Roman Catholic Management,* Dublin: Catholic Primary School Management Association.

Cullen, P. (2000), *Refugees and Asylum Seekers in Ireland,* Cork: Cork University Press.

Daly, T. (2001), 'Pedagogy and Disability: Insights from Action Research', *Irish Educational Studies,* vol. 20, pp. 107–23.

Deignan, A. (2000), 'The Retrieval of Natural Law Theory: Grounds for an Essentialist Perspective on Homosexuality', Dublin: unpublished thesis in equality studies, University College Dublin.

Department of Education (1965), *Rules for National Schools,* Dublin: Stationery Office.

Department of Education (1966), *Investment in Education: Report of the Survey Team,* Dublin: Stationery Office.

Department of Education (1969), *Leaving Certificate Home Economics (Social and Scientific),* Dublin: Stationery Office.

Department of Education (1970), *Educational Facilities for the Children of Itinerants,* Dublin: Stationery Office.

Department of Education (1971), *Curaclam na Bunscoile/Primary School Curriculum,* Dublin: Stationery Office.

Department of Education (1972), *The Education of Children Who Are Handicapped by Impaired Hearing,* Dublin: Stationery Office.

Department of Education (1993), *Guidelines on Countering Bullying Behaviour in Primary and Post-primary Schools,* Dublin: Stationery Office.

Department of Education (1994), *Guidelines for Schools,* Dublin: Stationery Office.

Department of Education (1995), *Charting our Education Future: White Paper on Education,* Dublin: Stationery Office.

Department of Education and Science (no date), *Information Booklet for Schools on Asylum Seekers,* Dublin: Department of Education and Science.

Department of Education and Science (1998a), *Promoting Gender Equality in the '90s,* Dublin: Stationery Office.

Department of Education and Science (1998b), *Green Paper: Adult Education in an Era of Lifelong Learning,* Dublin: Stationery Office.

Department of Education and Science (1999a), *Social, Personal and Health Education. Primary School Curriculum,* Dublin: Stationery Office.

Department of Education and Science (1999b), *Revised Primary School Curriculum,* Dublin: Stationery Office.

Department of Education and Science (1999c), 'Changes Will Relieve Significant Fundraising Pressures on Local Community', press release, 10 January 1999.

Department of Education and Science (1999d), *Civic, Social and Political Education (CSPE) Syllabus,* Dublin: Department of Education and Science.

Department of Education and Science (1999e), *Support for Post-Primary Schools Enrolling Traveller Children, Circular Letter M43/99,* Dublin: Department of Education and Science.

Department of Education and Science (1999f), *Ready to Learn: White Paper on Early Childhood Education,* Dublin: Stationery Office.

Department of Education and Science (2000a), *Learning for Life: White Paper on Adult Education,* Dublin: Stationery Office.

Department of Education and Science (2000b), *Social, Personal and Health Education, Junior Cycle,* Dublin: Stationery Office.

Department of Education and Science (2000c), *Junior Certificate Religious Education Syllabus,* Dublin: Stationery Office.

Department of Education and Science (2000d), *Statistical Report 1998/99,* Dublin: Stationery Office.

Department of Education and Science (2000e), *Exploring Masculinities: A Programme in Personal and Social Development for Transition Year and Senior Cycle Boys and Young Men,* Dublin: Department of Education and Science.

Department of Education and Science (2001), *Leaving Certificate Home Economics (Social and Scientific) Syllabus,* Dublin: Stationery Office.

Department of Education and Science (2002a), *Financial Support for Further and Higher Education, 2002/2003,* Dublin: Department of Education and Science.

Department of Education and Science (2002b), *Promoting Anti-Racism and Interculturalism in Education,* Dublin: Department of Education and Science.

Department of Education and Science (2002c), *Guide for Mature Students,* Dublin: Department of Education and Science.

Department of Education and Science (2002d), *Guidelines on Traveller Education in Primary Schools,* Dublin: Stationery Office.

Department of Education and Science (2002e), *Guidelines on Traveller Education in Second-Level Schools,* Dublin: Stationery Office.

Department of Education and Science (2003a), *Summary of All Initiatives Funded by the Department to Help Alleviate Educational Disadvantage,* Dublin: Department of Education and Science (Social Inclusion Unit).

Department of Education and Science (2003b), *Supporting Equity in Higher Education,* Dublin: Department of Education and Science.

Department of Education and Science (2003c), *Looking at Our School: An Aid to Self-Evaluation in Primary Schools,* Dublin: Stationery Office.

Department of Education and Science (2003d), *Looking at Our School: An Aid to Self-Evaluation in Second-Level Schools,* Dublin: Stationery Office.

Department of Health and Children (2000), *The National Children's Strategy: Our Children – Their Lives,* Dublin: Stationery Office.

Department of Social, Community and Family Affairs (2000), *Review of the One-Parent Family Payment,* Dublin: Stationery Office.

Devine, D., Kenny, M. and McNeela, E. (2004), 'Experiencing Racism in the Primary School: Children's Perspectives', in J. Deegan, D. Devine and A. Lodge (eds.), *Primary Voices: Equality, Childhood and Diversity in Irish Primary Schools,* Dublin: Institute of Public Administration.

Dillon, M. (1999), *Catholic Identity: Balancing Reason, Faith and Power,* Cambridge: Cambridge University Press.

Drudy, S. and Lynch, K. (1993), *Schools and Society in Ireland,* Dublin: Gill & Macmillan.

Drudy, S. and Uí Cathain, M. (1999), *Gender Equality in Classroom Interaction,* Maynooth: Education Department, National University of Ireland, Maynooth.

Duffy, M. (1993), 'Integration or Segregation: Does it Make a Difference? A Study of Equality Issues Relating to the Education of Disabled Girls', Dublin: unpublished thesis in equality studies, University College Dublin.

Egan, M. (2000), 'Students Who Have Down Syndrome: A Study of Their School Placements, Educational Supports and Parental Evaluation of Their Education', Maynooth: unpublished thesis in education, National University of Ireland, Maynooth.

Egan, O. (ed.) (1996), *Women Staff in Irish Colleges,* Cork: Higher Education Equality Unit.

Egan, O. (ed.) (1997), *Minority Ethnic Groups in Higher Education in Ireland, Proceedings of Conference Held in St. Patrick's College, Maynooth, 27th September,* Cork: Higher Education Equality Unit.

Equality Authority, IBEC, ICTU and CIF (2000), *Anti-Racism in the Workplace Resource Pack,* Dublin: Equality Authority.

Equality Authority (2001), *Equality News,* Spring issue, Dublin: Equality Authority.

Equality Authority (2002a), *Implementing Equality for Lesbians, Gays and Bisexuals,* Dublin: Equality Authority.

Equality Authority (2002b), *Implementing Equality for Older People,* Dublin: Equality Authority.

Eurostat (2001), 'Women and Science: Women Hold Less Than One-Third of Posts in Higher Education, Teaching and Public Research', news release no. 118, 8 November 2001, Luxembourg.

Fahey, T., Fitzgerald, J. and Maître, B. (1998), 'The Economic and Social Implications of Demographic Change', *Journal of the Statistical and Social Inquiry Society of Ireland,* vol. 27, no. 5, pp. 185–222.

Fanning, B., Loyal, S. and Staunton, C. (2000), *Asylum Seekers and the Right to Work in Ireland,* Dublin: Irish Refugee Council.

Fanning, B., Veale, A. and O'Connor, D. (2001), *Beyond the Pale: Asylum-Seeking Children and Social Exclusion in Ireland,* Dublin: Irish Refugee Council.

Farrell, S. (1995), *Legislation, Disability and Higher Education: A Comparative Study, Europe and the USA,* Dublin: AHEAD.

Faughnan, P. and Woods, M. (2000), *Lives on Hold: Seeking Asylum in Ireland,* Dublin: Social Science Research Centre, University College Dublin.

Fearon, K. (1996), 'Moral and Ethical Issues in RSE: A Church of Ireland Perspective', in PSACICE (eds.), *Relationships and Sexuality Education in the Primary School,* Dublin: PSACICE.

Fleming, T. and Murphy, M. (1997), *College Knowledge: Power, Policy and Mature Student Experiences at University,* Maynooth: Centre for Adult and Community Education, National University of Ireland, Maynooth.

Finkelstein, V. and Stuart, O. (1996), 'Developing New Services', in G. Hales (ed.), *Beyond Disability: Towards an Enabling Society,* London: Sage.

Flynn, M. (2002), 'Equality of Access: A Basic Right for All', paper given at the Educational Studies Association of Ireland Annual Conference, 21–23 March 2002, Trinity College, Dublin.

Forest, M. (1991), 'It's About Relationships', in L.H. Meyer, C.A. Peck and L. Brown (eds.), *Critical Issues in the Lives of People with Severe Disabilities,* Baltimore, MD: Paul H. Brookes.

Foyle Friend (1999), *The Experiences of Lesbian, Gay and Bisexual People at School in the Northwest of Ireland,* Derry: Foyle Friend.

Galligan, Y. (2000), *The Development of Mechanisms to Monitor Progress in Achieving Gender Equality in Ireland. Report Commissioned by the Department of Justice, Equality and Law Reform,* Dublin: Stationery Office.

Gardner, H. (1985), *Frames of Mind: The Theory of Multiple Intelligences,* New York: Basic Books.

Gay HIV Strategies & NEXUS (1999), *Education: Lesbian and Gay Students,* Dublin: Gay HIV Strategies & NEXUS.

Glendenning, D. (1999), *Education and the Law,* Dublin: Butterworths.

GLEN/NEXUS (1995), *Poverty, Lesbians and Gay Men: The Economic and Social Effects of Discrimination,* Dublin: Combat Poverty Agency.

Goodbody Economic Consultants (1998), *Study on the Economics of Childcare in Ireland. Report Commissioned by the Department of Justice, Equality and Law Reform on Behalf of the Partnership 2000 Expert Working Group on Childcare, December 1998,* Dublin: Stationery Office.

Gouldner, A.V. (1971), *The Coming Crisis of Western Sociology,* London: Heinemann.

Government of Ireland (2000), *National Development Plan 2000–2006,* Dublin: Stationery Office.

Gowran, S. (2000), 'Minority Sexualities in Education: The Experiences of Teachers', Dublin: unpublished thesis in equality studies, University College Dublin.

Griffin, K. (1997), 'Whither the Fourth R? A Perspective on the Future of Religion in the Primary School', in P. Hogan and K. Williams (eds.), *The Future of Religion in Irish Education,* Dublin: Veritas.

Hannan, D. and O'Riain, S. (1993), *Pathways to Adulthood in Ireland. Causes and Consequences of Success and Failure in Transitions Amongst Irish Youth, Paper No. 161,* Dublin: Economic and Social Research Institute.

Hannan, D.F. and Doyle, A. (2000), *Changing School to Work Transitions: Three Cohorts, ESRI Seminar Paper,* Dublin: Economic and Social Research Institute.

Hannan, D.F., Breen, R., Murphy, B., Watson, D., Hardiman, N. and O'Higgins, K. (1983), *Schooling and Sex Roles: Sex Differences in Subject Provision and Student Choice in Irish Post-Primary Schools. ESRI General Research Series, Paper No. 113,* Dublin: Economic and Social Research Institute.

Hannan, D.F., Smyth, E., McCullagh, J., O'Leary, R. and McMahon, D. (1996), *Coeducation and Gender Equality: Exam Performance, Stress and Personal Development,* Dublin: Oak Tree Press.

Hannan, D.F., McCabe, B. and McCoy, S. (1998), *Trading Qualifications for Jobs: Overeducation and the Irish Youth Labour Market,* Dublin: Oak Tree Press.

Harding, S. (1991), *Whose Science, Whose Knowledge? Thinking from Women's Lives,* Milton Keynes: Open University Press.

Healy, M. (1998), *Everything to Gain: A Study of the Third Level Allowance Scheme,* Dublin: Aontas.

HEEU (1996), *Mature Students in Higher Education,* Cork: Higher Education Equality Unit.

HEEU (1997), *Minority Ethnic Groups in Higher Education in Ireland,* Cork: Higher Education Equality Unit.

Hevey, D. (1993), 'The Tragedy Principle: Strategies for Change in the Representation of Disabled People', in J. Swain, V. Finkelstein, S. French and M. Oliver (eds.), *Disabling Barriers – Enabling Environments,* London: Sage.

Higher Education Authority (1995), *Interim Report of the Technical Working Group of the Steering Committee on the Future Development of Higher Education,* Dublin: Higher Education Authority.

Higher Education Authority (2003), *Provision of Undergraduate and Taught Postgraduate Education to Overseas Students in Ireland,* Dublin: Higher Education Authority.

Hogan, G. and Whyte, G. (eds.) (1994), *J. M. Kelly, The Irish Constitution,* 3rd ed., Dublin: Butterworths.

Hyland, A. (1989), 'The Multi-denominational Experience in the Irish National School System of Education', *Irish Educational Studies,* vol. 8, no. 1, pp. 89–114.

Hyland, A. (1996), 'Irish Experiments in Sharing in Education: Educate Together', in *Pluralism in Education: Conference Proceedings 1996,* Coleraine: Centre for the Study of Conflict, University of Ulster.

Inglis, T. (1998), *Moral Monopoly: The Rise and Fall of the Catholic Church in Modern Ireland,* 2nd ed., Dublin: UCD Press.

Inglis, T. (1999), *Lessons in Irish Sexuality,* Dublin: UCD Press.

Inglis, T. and Murphy, M. (1999), *No Room for Adults? A Study of Mature Students in University College Dublin,* Dublin: Social Science Research Centre and Adult Education Office, University College Dublin.

Integrate Ireland Language and Training (2002), 'Report on Activities 2002', unpublished report, Dublin: Integrate Ireland Language and Training.

INTO (1995), *Promoting School Attendance,* Dublin: INTO.

INTO (1998), *The Challenge of Diversity: Education Support for Ethnic Minority Children,* Dublin: INTO.

INTO (2001), *INTO Equality Committee Report 2001/2002,* Dublin: INTO.

INTO (2002), *INTO Intercultural Guidelines for Schools: Valuing Difference, Combating Racism, Promoting Inclusiveness and Equality,* Dublin: INTO.

Irish Refugee Council (2004), *Asylum-Seekers and Refugee Statistics in Ireland from January to June 2004* (available at www.irishrefugeecouncil.ie/stats.html, downloaded September 2004), Dublin: Irish Refugee Council.

Irish Traveller Movement (2000), *Annual Report,* Dublin: Irish Traveller Movement.

Keher, N. (1996), 'Academics Don't Have Babies: Maternity Leave Amongst Female Academics', in O. Egan (ed.), *Women Staff in Irish Colleges,* Cork: Higher Education Equality Unit.

Kennedy, R.E. (1973), *The Irish: Emigration, Marriage and Fertility,* Berkley, CA: University of California Press.

Kenny, M. (1997), *The Routes of Resistance: Travellers and Second Level Schooling,* Aldershot: Ashgate.

Kenny, M., McNeela, E., Shevlin, M. and Daly, T. (2000), *Hidden Voices: Young People with Disabilities Speak About Their Second Level Schooling,* Ballincollig, Co. Cork: The South West Regional Authority.

Keogh, A. (2000), 'Talking About the Other: A View of How Secondary School Pupils Construct Opinions About Refugees and Asylum-Seekers', in M. MacLachlan and M. O'Connell (eds.), *Cultivating Pluralism: Psychological, Social and Cultural Perspectives on a Changing Ireland,* Dublin: Oak Tree Press.

Keogh, A.F. and Whyte, J. (2002), 'Ethnic Minority Students' Needs and Experiences at Second Level', paper given at the Educational Studies Association of Ireland Annual Conference, 21–23 March 2002, Trinity College, Dublin.

Keogh, D. (1997), *Jews in Ireland,* Cork: Cork University Press.

Kitchin, R. and Mulcahy, F. (1999), *Disability, Access to Education, and Future Opportunities,* Dublin: Combat Poverty Agency.

Lodge, A. (1998), 'Gender Identity and Schooling: A Two-year Ethnographic Study of the Expression, Exploration and Development of Gender Identity in Seven to Nine Year Old Children in Their School Environment', Maynooth: unpublished thesis in education, National University of Ireland, Maynooth.

Lodge, A. (1999), 'First Communion in Carnduffy: A Religious and Secular Rite of Passage', *Irish Educational Studies,* vol. 18, pp. 210–22.

Lodge, A. (2004), 'Denial, Tolerance or Recognition of Difference? The Experiences of Minority Belief Parents in the Denominational Primary System', in J. Deegan, D. Devine and A. Lodge (eds.), *Primary Voices: Equality, Childhood and Diversity in Irish Primary Schools,* Dublin: Institute of Public Administration.

Lodge, A. and Lynch, K. (2000), 'Power: A Central Educational Relationship', *Irish Educational Studies,* vol. 19, pp. 46–67.

Lodge, A. and Lynch, K. (2001), 'The Diversity Deficit: Difficulties in the Recognition of Difference in Irish Schools', paper presented to the American Educational Research Association Annual Conference, Seattle, WA, 10–14 April.

Lynch, K. (1987), 'Dominant Ideologies in Irish Educational Thought:

Consensualism, Essentialism and Meritocratic Individualism', *Economic and Social Review,* vol. 18, no. 2.

Lynch, K. (1989), *The Hidden Curriculum: Reproduction in Education,* London: Falmer.

Lynch, K. (1994), 'Women Teach and Men Manage', in *Women for Leadership in Education,* Dublin: Education Commission of the Conference of Religious of Ireland.

Lynch, K. (1997), 'A Profile of Mature Students in Higher Education and an Analysis of Equality Issues', in R. Morris (ed.), *Mature Students in Higher Education,* Cork: Higher Education Equality Unit.

Lynch, K. (1999), *Equality in Education,* Dublin: Gill & Macmillan.

Lynch, K. and Connelly, A. (1996), 'Equality Before the Law', in *Report of the Constitution Review Group,* Dublin: Stationery Office.

Lynch, K. and Lodge, A. (1999), 'Essays on School', in K. Lynch, *Equality in Education,* Dublin: Gill & Macmillan.

Lynch, K. and Lodge, A. (2002), *Equality and Power in Schools: Redistribution, Recognition and Representation,* London: RoutledgeFalmer.

Lynch, K., Brannick, T., Clancy, P., Drudy, S. with Carpenter, A. and Murphy, M. (1999), *Points and Performance in Higher Education: A Study of the Predictive Validity of the Points System. Research Paper No. 4, Commission on the Points System,* Dublin: Stationery Office.

Lyons, M., Lynch, K., Close, S., Sheerin, E. and Boland, P. (2003), *Inside Classrooms: The Teaching and Learning of Mathematics in Social Context,* Dublin: Institute of Public Administration.

Mac an Ghaill, M. (1994), '(In)visibility: Sexuality, Race and Masculinity in the School Context', in D. Epstein (ed.), *Challenging Lesbian and Gay Inequalities in Education,* Buckingham: Open University Press.

MacGreil, M. (1996), *Prejudice in Ireland Revisited,* Maynooth: The Survey and Research Unit, Department of Social Studies, St Patrick's College, Maynooth.

MacLaughlin, J. (1995), *Travellers and Ireland: Whose Country? Whose History?,* Cork: Cork University Press.

Magee, C. (1994), *Teenage Parents: Issues of Policy and Practice,* Dublin: Irish Youthwork Press.

Malone, A. (2002), 'He Who Has the Bigger Stick Has the Better Chance of Imposing His Definition of Reality. Assimilation and Integration: International Students in a Second-Level School', Maynooth: unpublished thesis in education, National University of Ireland, Maynooth.

Mason, D. (1995), *Race and Ethnicity in Modern Britain,* Oxford: Oxford University Press.

Mason, M. (1990), 'Disability Equality in the Classroom – A Human Rights Issue', *Gender and Education,* vol. 2, no. 3, pp. 363–6.

McCarthy, M. (2001), *My Eyes Only Look Out: Experiences of Irish People of Mixed Race Parentage,* Dingle, Co. Kerry: Brandon.

McCashin, A. (1993), *Lone Parents in the Republic of Ireland: Enumeration, Description and Implications for Social Security,* Dublin: Economic and Social Research Institute.

McCashin, A. (1996), *Lone Mothers: A Local Study,* Dublin: Oak Tree Press.

McCashin, A. (1997), *Employment Aspects of Young Lone Parenthood in Ireland,* Dublin: Irish Youth Work Press.

McCoy, S., Doyle, A. and Williams, J. (1999), *1998 Annual School Leavers' Survey of 1996/97 Leavers,* Dublin: Department of Education and Department of Enterprise, Trade and Employment.

McDonagh, W. (2000), 'A Traveller Woman's Perspective on Education', in E. Sheehan (ed.), *Travellers: Citizens of Ireland,* Dublin: The Parish of the Travelling People.

McDonnell, P. (2002), 'Regulating Problem People: Discourses in Disability', public lecture, Equality Studies Centre, University College Dublin, 7 February 2002.

McGovern, A.M.F. (1990), 'Vietnamese Refugees in Ireland 1970–1989: A Case Study of Resettlement and Education', Dublin: unpublished thesis in education, Trinity College, Dublin.

McMinn, J. (2000), 'The Changers and the Changed: An Analysis of Women's Community Education Groups in the North and South of Ireland', Dublin: unpublished thesis in equality studies, Equality Studies Centre, University College Dublin.

McVeigh, R. (1995), *The Racialization of Irishness: Centre for Research and Documentation,* Belfast: Centre for Research and Documentation.

Milne, K. (1996), 'Relationship of the Church to Schools: Its Nature and Value', in *Pluralism in Education: Conference Proceedings 1996,* Coleraine: Centre for the Study of Conflict, University of Ulster.

Moane, G. (1995), 'Living Visions', in Í. O'Carroll and E. Collins (eds.), *Lesbian and Gay Visions of Ireland: Towards the Twenty-first Century,* London: Cassell.

Morgan, M. (2000), *Relationships and Sexuality Education: An Evaluation and Review of Implementation,* Dublin: Stationery Office.

Morgan, M., Hickey, B. and Kellaghan, T. (1997), *International Adult Literacy Survey: Results for Ireland,* Dublin: Stationery Office.

Morgan, V. (1991), *Gender Differentiation in Primary Schools: A Northern View,* Coleraine: Faculty of Education, University of Ulster.

Morris, R. (1997), *Mature Students in Higher Education,* Cork: Higher Education Equality Unit.

Mukherjee, S., Lightfoot, J. and Sloper, P. (2000), 'The Inclusion of Pupils with a Chronic Health Condition in Mainstream School: What Does It Mean for Teachers?', *Educational Research,* vol. 42, no. 1, pp. 59–72.

Mullally, S. (2001), 'Mainstreaming Equality in Ireland: A Fair and Inclusive Accommodation?', *Legal Studies,* vol. 21, pp. 99–115.

Murphy, B. (2000), *Support for the Educationally and Socially Disadvantaged: An Introductory Guide to Government Funded Initiatives in Ireland,* Cork: Education Department, University College Cork.

Murphy, C. and Adair, L. (2002), *Untold Stories: Protestants in the Republic of Ireland 1922–2002,* Dublin: Liffey Press.

Murphy, G. (2001), 'Towards Developing School Attendance Strategies', Maynooth: unpublished action research study completed in part fulfilment of the requirements for the Higher Diploma in Educational Management, Education Department, National University of Ireland, Maynooth.

Murray, M.B. (2000), 'Inclusive Education for Refugee Children: Issues to Be Addressed', Dublin: unpublished thesis in equality studies, University College Dublin.

National Council for Curriculum and Assessment (1999), *Special Educational Needs: Curriculum Issues,* Dublin: National Council for Curriculum and Assessment.

National Council for Curriculum and Assessment (2001), *Social, Personal and Health Education. Junior Certificate Guidelines for Teachers,* Dublin: Stationery Office.

NALA (National Adult Literacy Association) (2001), *Access and Participation in Adult Literacy Schemes* (www.nala.ie/publications/listing/20010525115737.html), Dublin: NALA.

National Co-ordinating Committee of the 1997 European Year Against Racism (1998), *Ireland Report,* Dublin: Department of Justice, Equality and Law Reform.

National Qualifications Authority of Ireland (2003), *Policies, Actions and Procedures for Access, Transfer and Progression for Learners,* Dublin: National Qualifications Authority of Ireland.

National Statistics Board (2004), *Best Practice for the Development and Implementation of Formal Data/Statistics Strategies in Government Department* (available at www.nsb.ie/publications/Data%20Strategy%20Guidelines.pdf), Dublin: National Statistics Board.

National Women's Council of Ireland (2001), *Women: Knowledge is Power.*

Women and Education. Report from the NWCI Millennium Project (www.nwci.ie/documents/education.doc), Dublin: National Women's Council of Ireland.

NESF (2001), *Lone Parents: National Economic and Social Forum Report No. 20,* Dublin: National Economic and Social Forum.

NESF (2002), A *Strategic Policy Framework for Equality Issues: National Economic and Social Forum Report No. 23,* Dublin: National Economic and Social Forum.

NESF (2003), *Equality Policies for Lesbian, Gay and Bisexual People: Implementation Issues: National Economic and Social Forum Report No. 27,* Dublin: National Economic and Social Forum.

Neville, G. (1996), 'The Lady Vanishes: Vertical Segregation and Barriers to Promotion for Female Academics', in O. Egan (ed.), *Women Staff in Irish Colleges,* Cork: Higher Education Equality Unit.

O'Carroll, Í. and Szalacha, L. (2000), A *Queer Quandary: The Challenges of Including Sexual Difference within the Relationships and Sexuality Education Programme,* Dublin: LEA/LOT.

O'Connell, J. (1998), *Travellers in Ireland: An Examination of Discrimination and Racism,* Dublin: Pavee Point.

OECD (1991), *Reviews of National Policies for Education – Ireland,* Paris: OECD.

OECD (1995), *Economic Survey of Ireland,* Paris: OECD.

OECD (1998), *Human Capital Investment: An International Comparison,* Paris: OECD.

OECD (2000), *Education at a Glance: OECD Indicators,* Paris: OECD.

OECD (2002), *Education at a Glance: OECD Indicators,* Paris: OECD.

O'Keeffe, M. (1997), 'Charting Developments in Educational Provision for Visually Impaired Students in Ireland (1970–1997)', Maynooth: unpublished thesis in education, National University of Ireland, Maynooth.

Oliver, M. (1990), *The Politics of Disablement,* Basingstoke, Hampshire: Macmillan Education Ltd.

O'Riordan, C. (2001), 'NALA Responds to White Paper on Adult Education', *NALA Journal,* Autumn 2001, pp. 20–1.

Quinn, G. (1993), 'Disability Discrimination Law in the United States', in G. Quinn, M. McDonagh and C. Kimber (eds.), *Disability Discrimination Law in the United States, Australia and Canada,* Dublin: Oak Tree Press in association with the National Rehabilitation Board.

Randles, E. (1996), 'Relationship of the Church to Schools: Its Nature and Value', in *Pluralism in Education: Conference Proceedings 1996,* Coleraine: Centre for the Study of Conflict, University of Ulster.

Richardson, V. (2000), *Young Mothers: A Study of Young Single Mothers in Two*

Communities. A Study Commissioned by the Vincentian Partnership for Justice, Dublin: Social Science Research Centre, University College Dublin.

Rose, K. (1994), *Diverse Communities: The Evolution of Lesbian and Gay Politics in Ireland,* Cork: Cork University Press.

Ryan, M.M. (1998), 'The Case for Third Age Intergenerational Education: An Examination of the Demographic and Social Reasons for Establishing a Pilot Project', Dublin: unpublished thesis in equality studies, University College Dublin.

Sailor, W. (1991), 'Community School: An Essay', in L.H. Meyer, C.A. Peck and L. Brown (eds.), *Critical Issues in the Lives of People with Severe Disabilities,* Baltimore, MD: Paul H. Brookes.

Secondary Education Committee Grants Section (1999), *Grants,* information leaflet, Dublin: Secondary Education Committee, Grants Section, Belgrave House, Rathmines.

Sherlock, H. (2002), 'Recognition of Foreign Qualifications', paper presented to the Annual Conference of the Educational Studies Association of Ireland, Trinity College, Dublin, 21–23 March.

Shevlin, M. and O' Moore, A.M. (1999), 'Fostering Positive Attitudes Towards Young People with the Severest Disabilities', Irish Educational Studies, vol. 18, pp. 165–79.

Skilbeck, M. (2002), *The University Challenged: A Review of International Trends and Issues with Particular Reference to Ireland,* Dublin: Higher Education Authority.

Smith, D. (1987), *The Everyday World as Problematic: A Feminist Sociology,* Milton Keynes: Open University Press.

Smyth, E. (1999), *Do Schools Differ? Academic and Personal Development among Pupils in the Second-Level Sector,* Dublin: Oak Tree Press in association with Economic and Social Research Institute.

Smyth, E. (2001), 'Gender Differentiation in Education and Early Labour Market Transitions: A Comparative Analysis', CATEWE individual research paper, Mannheim: Mannheimer Zentrum für Europäische Sozialforschung, Universität Mannheim.

Smyth, E. and Hannan, D. (2000), 'Education and Inequality', in B. Nolan, P.J. O'Connell and C.T. Whelan (eds.), *Bust to Boom: The Irish Experience of Growth and Inequality,* Dublin: Institute of Public Administration.

Special Education Review Committee (1993), *Report,* Dublin: Stationery Office.

Spender, D. (1982), *Invisible Women: The Schooling Scandal,* London: Writers and Readers.

Stanworth, M. (1983), *Gender and Schooling: A Study of Sexual Divisions in the Classroom,* London: Hutchinson.

129

Steer, J. (1996), 'Educate Together: Pluralism in Primary Education in the Republic of Ireland', in *Pluralism in Education: Conference Proceedings 1996*, Coleraine: Centre for the Study of Conflict, University of Ulster.

Stevens, P.E. and Morgan, S. (1999), 'Health of Lesbian, Gay, Bisexual and Transgender Youth', *Journal of Child and Family Nursing*, vol. 2, no. 4, pp. 237–51.

Task Force on Autism (2001), *Draft Report*, Dublin: Department of Education and Science.

Task Force on Dyslexia (2001), *Report*, Dublin: Department of Education and Science.

Task Force on the Traveller Community (1996), *Report*, Dublin: Stationery Office.

TED/CEDR (2003), *Celebrating Difference: Promoting Equality. Intercultural Education in the Irish Primary Classroom*, Limerick: Curriculum Development Unit, Mary Immaculate College.

Tobin, K. (1993), 'Target Students', in B. Fraser (ed.), *Research Implications for Science and Mathematics Teachers*, vol. 1, Perth: National Key Centre for School Science and Mathematics, Curtin University of Technology.

Tovey, H. and Share, P. (2000), *A Sociology of Ireland*, Dublin: Gill & Macmillan.

Trainees at St Joseph's Training Centre (2000), 'Young Travellers' Experience of Education', in E. Sheehan (ed.), *Travellers: Citizens of Ireland*, Dublin: Parish of the Travelling People.

Travelling People Review Body (1983), *Report*, Dublin: Stationery Office.

Teachers' Union of Ireland (1990), *Equality of Opportunity in Teaching*, Dublin: Teachers' Union of Ireland.

Union of Students in Ireland (2004), 'Student Attitudes Towards Lesbian, Gay and Bisexual Students in Third Level Education, 2004', Dublin: unpublished research report, Union of Students in Ireland.

VTOS (2002), *Guide for Mature Students: Entry to Full-time Third-level Courses*, Dublin: VTOS.

Wallace, W. (2001), 'A Term of Abuse', *Times Education Supplement*, 19 January 2001, pp. 9–10.

Warren, L. and O'Connor, E. (1999), *Stepping Out of the Shadows: Women in Educational Management in Ireland*, Dublin: Oak Tree Press.

Watney, S. (1991), 'School's Out', in D. Fuss (ed.), *Inside/Out: Lesbian Theories, Gay Theories*, London: Routledge.

Weiner, G. (1994), *Feminisms in Education: An Introduction*, Buckingham: Open University Press.

White, J. (1975), *Minority Report: The Protestant Community in the Irish Republic*, Dublin: Gill & Macmillan.

Witcher, H. (1984), 'Personal and Professional: A Feminist Approach', in J. Whyte, R. Deem, L. Kant and M. Cruickshank (eds.), *Girl Friendly Schooling,* London: Methuen.

Young, I.M. (1990), *Justice and the Politics of Difference,* Princeton: Princeton University Press.

Younger, M. and Warrington, M. (1996), 'Differential Achievement of Girls and Boys at GCSE: Some Observations from the Perspective of One School', *British Journal of Sociology of Education,* vol. 17, no. 3, pp. 299–313.

Zappone, K. (2003), *Re-thinking Identity: The Challenge of Diversity,* Belfast: Equality Commission for Northern Ireland and Northern Ireland Human Rights Commission; Dublin: The Equality Authority and Human Rights Commission; and London: Commission for Racial Equality, Disability Rights Commission, and Equal Opportunities Commission.